Intense, beautiful and deeply moving, *Hook: A M[...]* story about survival of the streets, survival of th[...] writing. I won't stop thinking about this book i[...]

—CRYSTAL WILKINSON, AUTHOR OF *WATER STREET*

In a cerebral epistolary form full of gritty, thick description, Randall Horton has given us a meditation on life in America's margins that lyrically splits the difference between memoir and treatise, diagnostic and self-refraction. The hard blues and abstracted truths delineated within speak in a harrowing and omniscient tongue about the fates and the furies that bewilder and bedevil the complex human equations who pockmark the nation's race, gender, and class inequities. Only a poet of the first rank could have made the social reporting and analytical bent of this opus sing with such brio and bravura. In this moment of Black Lives under the gun being said to suddenly matter, Horton has supplied us with fresh, in-depth reports from the gods and semi-urges who haunt the details.

—GREG TATE, AUTHOR OF *FLYBOY IN THE BUTTERMILK*

The tale many African American writers tell is often about survival. In the 21st Century one must ask how long the lash? How large the prison? Randall Horton breaks free in his memoir *Hook* just in time to remind our nation that there are many black souls in need of salvation. Black men are not missing or absent. We simply struggle to control our own narrative. Horton in *Hook* gives us letters of confessions without envelopes. He has written a book that tries to convince the human spirit to stay above water. We are not sinners but beautiful swimmers refusing to drown. *Hook* is the memoir Etheridge Knight might have written on those nights when a haiku became nothing but a shank. When memoir turns to flesh there should be baptism and truth. I continue to be haunted by the words of Randall Horton's father—"Please, please give me my boy back. His is a life worth saving." *Hook* is a book worth reading and might bless our eyes. Lord, after the long rain of tears, we need to see a rainbow. A fire burns in Horton's hands. *Hook* should be the next book you read.

—E. ETHELBERT MILLER, LITERARY ACTIVIST AND BOARD CHAIR OF THE INSTITUTE FOR POLICY STUDIES

HOOK

HOOK

A MEMOIR

BY

RANDALL HORTON

New York, New York

HOOK: A Memoir
© 2015 Randall Horton

ISBN-13: 978-0-9887355-6-9

Cover design by Michael Miller

Published in the United States of America by Augury Books. All rights reserved. For reprouction inquiries or other information, please visit AuguryBooks.com

First Edition

FOR
JESSE JAMES JACKSON

CONTENTS

Journal Note to [SELF]: Dear Reader, Follow the North Star   xiii

Because Hook Doesn't Exist   xv

Exordium   xix

One: Origin of Lxxxx   1

Two: Louder than All Sound Ever Created   9
    Journal Note to [SELF]: Open Door—   15
    Excerpt I: The Real HU   17
       The Real Howard University
       Off Campus   21
       The Collective   23
       Earthworks, the Mecca   25
       Move to Harvard Street   28
       Exodus   32

Three: Connections and Disconnections   37

Four: Process and Ending Point   43
    Journal Note to [SELF]: Look See   47
    Excerpt II: Slippin' into Darkness   49
       Destiny and Fate
       Living the Dream   55
       Contact   62
       Deception   65
       Theatre of the Absurd   68

Five: Space and Time   77

Six: Same Sky, Different Worlds   85

Seven: Flipping the Script   101
    Journal Note to [SELF]: A Tale of Time   105
    Excerpt III: All In—   107
       Jo-Jo, Punkin, and Me
       Invisible Man, Too   114
       Betrayal   116

Only by the Grace   120
Hindsight   126
Lxxxx Private Journal: Only by the Grace, Too   129
Coming Clean   139
The State   142
Old School and Black   146
Father, Forgive Me   151

Eight: Female Prison   159

Nine: Prison Industrial Complex   165
Journal Note to [SELF]: Burn the House   167
Exceprt IV: A Brand New Morning   169
TROSA
Return to DC   174
The Lake's Reflection   181

Ten: One More Thing   187

Coda   189

Acknowledgements   193

About the Author   195

In the middle of the journey of our life,
I came to myself, in a dark wood,
where the direct way was lost.
It is a hard thing to speak of, how wild,
harsh and impenetrable that wood was,
so that thinking of it recreates the fear.
It is scarcely less bitter than death: but,
in order to tell of the good that I found there,
I must tell of the other things I saw there.

—DANTE ALIGHIERI, *THE INFERNO (CANTO I),* TRANS. JOSEPH SULTANA

I feel the need to reaffirm all of it, the whole unhappy territory and all
the things loved and unlovable in it, for it is all part of me.

—RALPH ELLISON, *INVISIBLE MAN*

JOURNAL NOTE TO [SELF]:

DEAR READER, FOLLOW THE NORTH STAR

Erratic remnants of starlight singe uniform rooftops within a five-block radius. Adjusting our lens farther down into the scope of an urban city, outlines of humans mechanized by societal structures disappear into a hole in the ground, and are erased. Calibrating the audio reveals decompressing diesel brakes trudging up the Upper West Side, car engines idling, even loud Pepito selling THE TIMES across from the bodega. Location only matters because of conditions that create location. We discourse in dualism, operating under the assumption conditions run parallel, that space interrelates through distant memory: Langston and Gwendolyn, Neruda and Morejón. Hear the echo on the overground railroad—part metaphor, part homage to Harriet, who would have freed more if they'd known they were in bondage. Perhaps we can be new-millennium Harriets, create renegade languages, rescuing status quo from language bondage, as in, *them shackled and don't even know it.* Traveling through black spat night, snaking around corners onto new corners, refusing a final destination. Tenements seep through the train's synthetic glass pane. 125TH STREET in block lettering. AMERICA appears over the leaf breastplate of a man in solid blue dress. Uniformity along the isles, everybody facing north as if something unknown awaits. *Amazing grace,* the homeless man in the corner with his hand cupped for change belts, *how sweet the sound* no one hears, only the drone....

BECAUSE HOOK DOESN'T EXIST

2009 — HARLEM, NY

Answer the phone at 10:00 p.m. Offer a reserved *hello* on a nebulous
night filled with pallid snow in Harlem. Respond with *okay*. Listen.
Be attentive when you learn he died in a hail of gunfire at the
intersection of Minnesota Avenue and East Capitol Street in the
nation's capital. After thinking, *that's fucked up*, thank your old
college roommate for calling. Ignore that he greeted you as Hook,
the nickname you went by in the streets. Hang up. You can and you
can't believe the truth simultaneously. Write D-I-S-C-O in your leather
journal. Maybe this will immortalize the image. You will never forget
him, but you have already forgotten Hook.

    Before the blackbirds' echo bangs against your windowsill,
wake up. Go directly to the mahogany desk between two windows.
Sit in the brown swivel chair. Stare at the building opposite your
building. Rearrange papers that don't need rearranging—twice. Open
your journal to the name written last night. DISCO. Remember the
cell doors opening after serving eighteen months for three felonies in
Fairfax County Adult Detention Center. Five hours after that release,
meet Disco wheeling an ATM through your basement on a handcart.
Out of the wall, with metal chain and pickup truck, he had pulled the
money machine. He did that. This is your introduction.

    Turn on the computer. Type THEODORE BLANDFORD in the
search box. Click the magnifying glass. Expect to be surprised even
though you know what the results will bring. Don't be surprised
when you scroll to MARYLAND DOUBLE HOMICIDE SUSPECT SHOT, KILLED
IN DC. One lone bird outside your window flies backwards at an
indeterminate rate of speed while the world moves forward. The bird
is red. Look for balance in the oddity. Note that DOUBLE HOMICIDE is
five syllables. Five deliberate pauses before, *damn*. Remember you
knew the suspect/shooter/killer. Suspend *court* in your imagination.
Add four indeterminate words to formulate the phrase *hold court in
the streets*. This is how he will die: *holding court in the streets*. Prophetic.
After reading that the now-deceased wife had wanted a divorce,
deduce it was because of drugs. Visualize the wife and sister just
before death in their double-wide. Try to make sense of blood spilled
on the carpet. The red is deafening. Scream. Wait for the buzz to
stop, because someone rang the wrong buzzer. There is always an
echo after the buzzing. Even after it buzzes again, don't answer. It

is not for you. Keep reading the online article, but more specifically, the phrases FORCIBLE ENTRY and PROTECTIVE ORDER. Acknowledge that your friend was a suspect in his first wife's murder, too. A dead body in the trunk.

Two days later while driving to school to teach, call Short Man, because it takes that long to find someone to talk about tragedy. Tell Short Man, who is a barber and has ten years behind razor wire tucked in his memory, what happened. Agree in unison that prison will turn the brain into a *hum*. Agree again that prison taught you to be a better criminal—though you both digress. Both of you understand the term *anomaly* but admit that Disco was a composite of many men who never learned to be a man. You will then ask the question for the first time. *Why?*

Return back home from New Haven before rush-hour traffic begins to bottleneck the Cross County Parkway. Dig through the closet for the first version of your memoir. DISCO ROLLED THE SAFE OUT OF THE DEPARTMENT STORE, the first lines of the paragraph read. Go to the next page, where HE LOVES TO PULL THE TRIGGER OF A GUN MORE THAN HE LOVES TOUCHING THE TORSO OF A WOMAN. Flip to the page where he and his sister distribute lead bullets through the windshield and THE IMPRESSIONS OF CIRCULAR HOLES WHEN THE DISCARDED LEAD PIERCES THE GLASS ARE SWIFT AND PRONOUNCED. The body is a question mark.

He tried to run over the wife with his truck and then threatened her with a claw hammer. She told the police. Ask yourself why this sign didn't signify violence. What theory would Ferdinand de Saussure classify this under? Put the manuscript back in the closet. Don't beat yourself up because you knew he was a killer and said nothing to nobody. Forget the double negative your mom would correct you on, and tell yourself it's nature versus nurture. Justify your silence in saying that the world you once lived in was filled with silence and mayhem. That's why they called you Hook. Don't block Audre Lorde's *your silence will not protect you* from your mind. Pretend this is penance.

Wake up the next morning. Go back to the computer. Press any key to erase the black screen. Ignore the blackbirds outside your window while telling yourself this is the last time. You need to forget, but before you do, one more search. Click INMATE VIOLENT DEATHS IN THE NEWS. A flutter of blackbirds appear suspended in animation at the top right corner of the web page. Ignore them but then don't. Tell yourself this is not karma Edgar Allen Poe style.

He did not want her to leave. She wanted him to go. Said he needed treatment. Think back to twelve-step literature that cautions about the thirteenth step: sexual fraternization with people inside the circle. Feel confident in assuming she was a recovering addict and understood addictive behavior. Two addicts don't make a right. Tell yourself this.

Read about the interaction with police who failed to notice the inevitable. Admit the judicial system is failing to protect women. I AM VICTIM was tattooed on her forehead, yet she remained invisible to the patriarchs—the ones sworn to protect and serve. Ask yourself, *does his death matter more than the victim's death.* Convince yourself the race never stops running, that memory will eat you alive. Say, *I am a changed man,* but no one will hear you. Get back in the bed. Pull the covers over your face. Remember to dream. Forget Hook. Wake up tomorrow and feel guilty again.

EXORDIUM

The smear of incarceration is a difficult stain to erase within a society demanding forgiveness but collectively unwilling to forgive. Every day some*thing* or some*one* reminds us that we cannot outrun the past, nor can we delete memory, which often offers the building blocks to language.

Upon release from Roxbury Correctional Institute in 2000, I was looking for the right words to adequately articulate a complicated memory accumulated through drugs, addiction, and homelessness. The poetry of Etheridge Knight made terrible beauty out of the ugly; his love poems reminded me of my own relationships with street-wise women who used their bodies as a commodity. What I saw underneath the layers of hardness in his poems was the gentle poet who reimagined urban life and rearranged those images into poems.

Along with poets John Murillo, Reginald Dwayne Betts, and Marcus Jackson, I now help form THE SYMPHONY: THE HOUSE THAT ETHERIDGE BUILT, a homage to the work and memory of Knight. Part lecture, part poetic suite, it is an overture to Knight and an introduction to the voices of his literary descendants. This weekend we are doing a workshop and reading at Park University in Kansas City, Missouri. Not more than six months ago, we were at the University of South Carolina to do a reading and conduct a workshop at a juvenile detention center with over three hundred black and brown faces—a figure that only helped validate the narrative of people of color overcrowding prisons. Park is inviting THE SYMPHONY to conduct a poetry workshop with high school students from across the region, hoping to attract more English majors to the university. We will read later tonight to students at Paseo High School; however, that is not on my mind at the moment.

Instead, I am more occupied with Lxxxx, who once said I carried a dead weight on my shoulders, that there was a lead chain in my walk, rattling of prison. She, too, had seen the inside of razor wire and brick, understood how penitentiary time can squeeze a person's brain until it's nothing more than a *hum*.

Back when I was completing course work for my doctorate at SUNY Albany, Lxxxx had just returned to school upon finishing a three-year prison sentence. She became a trusted friend because she understood more than most what it was like to live with the lock and release of a cell door. I met her at a time when I needed to learn how to be a friend to women. I had purposely avoided any type of intimate relationships when I got out of prison because I knew I needed to work on Randall, the human being. History had taught me I was a flawed individual who had failed to engage people with compassion. Instead, I'd always looked to get over, especially with women. I could not conceive of being in an intimate relationship until I had completed every piece of education that would allow people the opportunity to forgive me for my past transgressions. Although Lxxxx had a boyfriend at the time, we found time to talk, compare our lives, and dream of something bigger than the prison world we had come from. When she graduated, Lxxxx went back to New York City to continue her studies in graduate school at Lehman College. I eventually received my doctorate and accepted a tenure-track position as Assistant Professor of English at the University of New Haven.

A month before I am to travel to Kansas City, Lxxxx's friend calls to inform me that Lxxxx has been arrested. She unknowingly gave a friend a ride under FBI surveillance, and when they stopped the car, the authorities found thirty-six kilos of cocaine—a white lady narcotic I am all too familiar with—in her friend's suitcase, and just like that, Lxxxx is back inside prison. We can hope that the authorities will exercise discretion in handling her situation, but until then, Lxxxx will have to wait in a cell while the legal system works through her case.

We correspond via letters because her visiting list is full with family members. I ask Lxxxx to give me a sample of her childhood. Who was her rock? Growing up, how did she negotiate the streets? What were the mistakes? I tell Lxxxx that if she gives me a piece of her, I will, in return, share that stained memory I now carry on my shoulders. It is a journey we can explore together on dual planes so as not to repeat the madness. I keep wondering, what are the intersections that led us down similar paths to prison?

1

ORIGIN OF LXXXX

There are certain situations about the past and family that are hard to discuss. For years I've been trying to forget, but as you say, one cannot shake the past; it will affect you—haunt you. My childhood was not bad. I'm the youngest of four children and my dad's only biological daughter. My mother is nine years older than him. He helped her raise my brother, Junior, and my sister, Toni. When my mother became pregnant with me, she decided to go to El Salvador and bring my oldest brother to the United States so he could live with us.

Randall, my dad has been an alcoholic forever—long before I was even thought of. My mom says he started drinking when his parents refused to let him join the military. They wanted him to work in the sugarcane fields and help the family. I don't know the whole story because I never asked him. He doesn't talk much and mostly talks to my mother. When my dad drinks, everyone around him becomes an enemy, a target for verbal abuse. If you didn't know him, you would be scared, but we knew he wasn't really capable of doing shit. We knew even though he was chasing my mother around the house with a knife, he wouldn't stab her; he enjoyed scaring her and showing his machismo in the house because no one in the real world respected his drunk ass. Sometimes when he got out of line and broke things, my mom would hit him and my brothers, too. This type of chaos was normal.

One day my mom threw bleach in his eyes because he was cursing and banging on the door trying to come in. One of the neighbors called the cops on her because my dad was knocking on everybody's door asking for water to clean his eyes. When the police came and questioned my mom, they ended up taking both of them to the precinct. She would not admit to anything and told the police he slipped and fell while she was mopping the kitchen floor. Eventually, they let my mom go because they got tired of her praying out loud and saying, *Dios mío son veinte años, que yo tengo soportando este animal, veinte años.* The cops in the precinct knew our family well—they knew my dad was a drunk; they knew my mom was screaming truth. Twenty years she had been dealing with my dad and supporting him; how dare they try to arrest her for defending herself? They let her go and made him spend the night in a cell. My mom never threw bleach in his eyes again.

There were times my dad would get so drunk she would not

let him in, and he would fall asleep in the hallway, so I would sneak him in or get a blanket and a pillow and lay with him on the steps. This would bother my mother, to see me out there with him, so she would let him in.

My siblings hated home, got married young, and left. By the time I was ten, it was just my parents and me. I was mad at being left behind. I wanted to live with Junior or Toni. I went to their houses often to visit until they started having kids, and then things changed. They had their own responsibilities, and they were strict, so I stopped going to their houses as much and started hanging in the streets. I could do whatever I wanted at home and didn't have to answer to anybody.

All this time, my dad still did not work, and when he did find a job, it never lasted. He always got fired because he would get drunk and couldn't work the next day. He often made money selling *coquitos*—you know, those fifty-cent and one-dollar ices that are coconut and cherry flavored—and he sold *piraguas* with the big block of ice. I think Americans call them snow cones. My father sold those for years until I didn't want him selling them anymore because I was embarrassed. I was twelve, and this is when life really began to change. I mean, my dad would insult my siblings, but never me. Lxxxx was always the exception.

Randall, the first time he flipped and hit me, it was right in front of my building, in front of everybody. Can you believe I hit him back? I was so ashamed and felt so guilty. I wanted to go to sleep for a very long time. That day I was home alone. Mami was at work, and I said fuck it and started popping pills she had for depression and a bunch of other medication she had lying around. I chased the pills with Bacardi my dad had stashed in my closet from one of his trips to Puerto Rico. This man would hide liquor in my closet to prevent my mom from throwing it away. Long story short, I stayed in a coma for days, and all my mom kept asking the doctors was, *Is she still a virgin?*—and I was.

When I woke up, all I remember is my mom crying and telling me, *No puedes decir la verdad because te mandan a un home, eso lo que tu quiere?* I couldn't tell the doctors the truth because they would take me away, put me in a home; then welfare would stop helping her, and it wasn't fair because my father didn't help, and she needed help from the welfare for food and rent. She told me what to say to the psychiatrist so they wouldn't take me away. I went to therapy for a couple of years, and every session was a lie. I never got the help I needed. After that, I didn't talk to my father for a year. When I did start back, it wasn't by choice—more like obligation. They had a fight, and my mother stabbed him. I needed to take him to the hospital and make sure he didn't say she did it. We made up a story and told the authorities he was robbed.

I was about thirteen or fourteen years old when I started working in a clothing store on Fordham Road. I didn't want my father washing cars and selling shit to take care of me, so I got a job. I tried to hustle crack, but that got boring quick. Being on Fordham exposed me to life quickly; everything moved fast over there. I wasn't used to it, but I learned. See, all the girls who worked on Fordham were pretty and used men to get whatever they wanted. It was there I learned how easy it was to manipulate men. Put it this way—at that point in my life, my sexual encounters with men weren't for love; they were because I knew I would get something out of them. I couldn't love, didn't know how.

Every week I gave my mom money, even though I only worked part time and made five dollars an hour. I did other things on the side, though, like transporting drugs on the Greyhound and trains. Transporting was like a side job for me. This is how I was really able to help my mom and dress myself. Having sex with older men was just another hustle. Of course, there were a couple of dudes I caught feelings for, but those feelings were never reciprocated. How could any man take a girl like me serious? I didn't even take myself serious.

At sixteen, I slipped and got pregnant. I was too afraid to tell my mom and dad, so I had an abortion. Life was already twisted, but that shit put my emotions on overdrive. My grades suffered behind all those dirty little secrets I kept. Aside from weed, I started drinking heavy, taking mescaline and acid, looking for anything to numb what I was feeling. When I got offered a trip to Panama for twenty stacks, I jumped at the opportunity. I didn't care what I had to swallow. I looked at the opportunity as a quick come up. I had never been arrested, so if I got bagged, I would get probation anyway. This is when I caught my first fed case, transporting H from Panama. You would think I would've slowed down after that case, but I got such a slap on the wrist, the system became a joke to me. Jail was a revolving door.

I caught an assault charge for beating up a dope fiend. Then I caught another case for robbery. That's when reality hit me, when I had to do time in prison. When I did those forty-two months, it was like a blessing in disguise because, at the rate I was going, I could've ended up dead or with AIDS. The physical distance from my family brought us all closer. We talked about everything, and they came to visit faithfully. There were times my dad only had enough for subway tokens, but he would still come to Rikers to see me.

Financially, times were tough, but my mother held things together. She continued to clean apartments and save money. My father washed cars and sold vegetables and fruit on the corner. He even worked construction for sixty-five dollars a day, working ten or twelve hours a day like a slave—but he did it. When I came home from prison I got Junior and my dad talking after several years of silence. Now they work together. Junior got my father a job as an elevator operator, and he's been working for the past ten years. That job has allowed him to buy my mom a house in Florida, and he takes care of her now.

Getting locked up this time around caught everyone by surprise—including me. I was going through a lot when I had my son. I never expected to be raising him by myself. I also never expected life as a college graduate to be so hard—that felony always came back to haunt me. I felt like I couldn't move past it even though I had come so far. I worked two jobs and still would have to dip and dab with shit to maintain. It was like I couldn't distance myself from the street life because the connections and opportunities were always there, even if it was only in a minor way. For example, I would sell weed to support my habit. I wasn't making no money off that shit. If I got my hands on anything else, it was extra, but never consistent. Never in a million years did I expect this to happen, especially not for no thirty-six kilos, but I put myself in this situation, being desperate and trusting muthafuckas too much. Thinking they my peoples and helping me when they really were using my ass and exploiting the situation I was in. They knew I needed money, knew I would bust a move if I had to to make some extra cash. I didn't need to know all the details all the time. That's exactly what happened that night. A ride to 42nd Street ended up being a move I didn't know about. I can only imagine how many times this guy did this to me without me knowing. Meanwhile, I'm thinking he's being generous whenever he throws me a few hundred for rent. In my sick mind, I thought I was doing the right thing. I wasn't fuckin' guys for money. I wasn't selling drugs in the street. I wasn't robbing anybody. I was driving from point A to point B to make some extra cash to feed my son.

I feel bad for my son because he did not ask to be here—

and my parents have been through enough shit with me. My mom and dad are too old to be dealing with him, and they don't have the energy, but they doin' it. Nobody else wanted to take him and, in retrospect, I'm glad. If anyone else were raising him, I would never see him, and he wouldn't know me. Randall, you asked, *What are the intersections that led us down similar paths to prison?* and I think the answer is obvious. We were both looking for a quick come up. Every time we set ourselves up for the rise, we fell into a deeper hole.

I've been thinking about you and your book. I hope it's going well and hope you will send me a peek? I've been reading J. California Cooper. I got my hands on two of her books and read them so quick that I wish I had taken my time. I read *Native Son* again, *Love* by Toni Morrison, and a few other books—fourteen to be exact—since April 13th. All the books have a common thread: choice, and a person's calling. Every protagonist has a problem figuring out his or her mission in life. I started to ask the women here if they knew what they were in this world for, and if they had a plan when they get out. None of them had an answer for me, not even me. Yeah, I have dreams, which is more than I can say for most women here, because it seems a lot of them stopped dreaming a long time ago, either when they caught their first bid or had their first child. It made me wonder about women and why we tend to stop believing in ourselves when life gets rough. There is something wrong mentally and spiritually with each one of us in here, an emptiness I can't explain. These white walls and gray trimmings have cast a shadow. I look beyond these walls, sometimes even beyond this life because I know there's more. Something inside me believes that this can't possibly be it. Maybe I'm a fool for still dreaming, but I can't help if I'm alive. These women don't seem alive to me, more like empty souls walking.

I'm teaching three women here how to read and write in English, and it is coming along beautifully. These women know so much, but they are embarrassed about mispronouncing words. It is very natural for them to feel self-conscious about their accents. I'm having a hard time finding reading material at the elementary level. I wrote to different agencies that donate books to inmates and requested workbooks and books to assist them with learning the fundamentals of English. I am waiting for a copy of *The House on Mango Street* by Sandra Cisneros. I think it would be perfect for them.

Anyway, how was your visit to Brooklyn? Hope you enjoyed the cold weather.

Lxxxx

2

LOUDER THAN ALL
SOUND EVER CREATED

Dear Lxxxx,

We script our lives on reaction rather than action, meaning daily life is always in response to, or a reply to, a command or demand. The world uses us in that way—the aftersound of oppression; we know this maxim, yet we become willing participants in our own commodification. The world does this—holds us down.

Then too, I've been thinking about the question you pose with regard to women and believing. Perhaps images and how we as a society nurture young women creates this insecurity. The American Dream chokes little girls insomuch as not all of them will be able to live up to ideal beauty as constructed by benefactors of the dominant narrative, those who dictate the ebb and flow of how we live. Beauty is a dangerous thing, and understand, brown and black women historically bear the weight of civilization in addition to their own weight, which can be daunting at times. But more than that, the male plays a role in this insecurity, especially in these so-called streets, by his rejection of the woman as equal counterpart and anything other than sexual object. We just wanna love and have some warm body love us back—objectification is a delicate balance.

In other words, I saw this objectification play out with men who dominated women to the point they broke their spirits and stole their sound. The women couldn't speak of their own oppression because they possessed no language to express the unimaginable, reminding me of Pudding and the streetwalker Sunshine. Sunshine adored Pudding so much she strolled around Logan Circle in DC every night selling the one commodity she knew well—herself. Here's the oxymoron: Sunshine never saw the light; darkness choked her to death. She never got to understand we are the shadows in the dark that Toni Morrison imagines. Our sound originates from the breaking of sound—and then again. Like life, language is only the beginning, and perhaps in its death, too, comes a new beginning, a new language.

Lxxxx, tonight I am imagining with exact description the six-by-nine cell you sleep in, in all its isolation, because this is something memory lets me reinvent: the gray cinderblock, the dull silver glow from the metal toilet. I have been thinking long and hard with regard to confinement and the bordering of color, and how we as a society imprison ourselves within the complexity of skin, as if human survival depends on this one specific thing. Of course, I could make a conscious effort to avoid color or not invade your

9

personal space when trying to make a parallelism, but history can be unforgiving in how the past (re)constructs the future, whether we acknowledge it or not. For some reason, I feel our histories and futures intersect insomuch as we come from the same memory. In other words, I have inhabited the cell door clang, and I can't escape the image of the pinstripe inmate constructed.

There it is, that word: *construct*, or *construction*, which is another word for confinement on someone else's terms—a sort of deliberate scaffolding. If I could go back to that initial moment after the formulation of earth—I'm talking about the first glorious sunrise after the big bang—have you ever wondered what that feeling could have been like? In the beginning, a delayed oceanic swirl lacked blue; foliage lacked green. Color had not begun. If only someone could have stopped progress at that precise moment.

But I guess you ponder why I choose your eyes to (re)imagine and confront my own confinement? To be straightforward, I have seen what you see, and I know color dictates how you move now and how you will move the next day, even in prison. Call it familiarity. So, one of the reasons color consumes me these days is because of the artist Margaret Bowland. I interviewed Margaret in February on the East Side of Manhattan for *Tidal Basin Review*, of which I am one of the editors. We were doing a feature on her paintings of an African American girl named J. What makes the work stunning and remarkable is that the model wears a light shadow of white, as if in whiteface, hinting at the concept W.E.B. Dubois coined in the twentieth century: double consciousness, chained to a way of seeing—a twoness that haunts the beholder. The models in Bowland's work are often depicted with cotton braided through their hair. At first glance, there is a beauty in what the artist captures; however, as one becomes drawn to J's eyes, the cultural pain and trauma, coupled with the sadness of this little girl never being able to live up to the image we as Americans have placed upon her, becomes an anvil. We revel in the beauty while drowning in our nation's damaging narration.

Bowland and I talked about how there is no rationalization for painting flesh—it's a concept based on how light illuminates a surface and projects an image. After leaving our interview, I began to think deeply about my own imprisonment in flesh, which I equate to color. When I did time in prison, I never contemplated being in a prison within a prison, and I wonder, have you ever thought about time in this manner? As for myself, I am constantly snapped back to the carcass I was, being eaten alive by the vulture time is. Until recently, I never considered how I swallowed the idea of color hook, line, and sinker. Lxxxx, we are all on life's preverbal hook, being reeled in by society's constructions. The next generation is counting on us to prepare a place much better, and I know we have failed—failed miserably. We war ourselves, we border ourselves, we kill ourselves. We are Latina, Black, Asian, White…and because of history, we never truly relinquish identity, so identity propels the narrative.

Consider the empirical evidence: a two-year-old boy in an apartment eight blocks from the detonation that killed four little girls in a church basement. All the girls wanted was to sing, and somebody stole their *li'l light of mine*. The picture of baby Jesus knocked off the hook, the apartment rattling from the detonation. I heard and felt that echo, a two-year-old boy being constructed to understand black and white, to choose a side. I was a construction before I came of age. For so long, all I could think about was vanishing from prison, not realizing I was imprisoned before incarceration, and I still languish behind invisible bars. I keep asking if this is the totality of my life. True, I am on the outside, but my inside is tangled up still. If life is the sum of history, how can I ever hope to escape this? Whether I choose to acknowledge the box or not, other people will, and there is no escaping this distinction. In other words, allow me to paraphrase Sartre for minute, who says that once man uttered the word *free*, man was no longer free because his need to be identified as "free" proved he was chained. I say I am free everyday, but really, how free am I?

Brooklyn is Brooklyn. I drove across the bridge to pick up artwork for the exhibit I am co-curating in the Catskills. The exhibit is titled *Uncle Remus Redux: Contemporary Visions of How Time Goes by Turns*, which is, at its core, a reimagining of African American folktales to unerase the erasure of a skewed narrative. I am going to send you some Nietzsche because, in reading *The Genealogy of Morals*, you will be able to draw interesting parallels to the lunacy of color and skin. What we can do is substitute Nietzsche's "aristocrat" with the fundamental core of people who benefited before the Industrial Revolution. I'm talking about those who facilitated the "stealing away" of those who were "stolen away" as what Nietzsche would call the "thing," which is conjoined to mal(us)—as in, the black, the people of melanin.

If Nietzsche's postulations are correct, and I most certainly suspect they are, then the moral tenets on which American society's foundation is based are a lie. Because we have evolved from the smallest minutia of indeterminate matter, a blip within the black slate of noise, to moniker ourselves as human analogously links us as a set entity, comprised of multihued voices, but still an entity—a collective object with myriad subsets, each bracketed subset essential to the tangential body as a whole. Only when we push against the grain, go against the dominant narrative, and dare to imagine (how dare we!)—then and only then will we stand on beauty's cliff and leap into a novel morning. Something unimaginable is what we should be imagining.

During the course of imaginative investigation, critical or creative, the writer has no choice but to confront *purpose*. As Audre Lorde famously said, *Your silence will not protect you*. See, I gotta talk about those who live underneath life and what we are permitted to read. Who will tell the story of the first time Pocketknife bent the hallway between algebra and English class, how I had to cop that hallway walk in the ninth grade, commodify it into my own? I wanted to lean, make my legs bow into a question mark and defy everything, just like Pocketknife.

Whenever I awaken from a nightmare induced by memory, *it begins where moonlight ends, slipping through the horizontal window, wraps each iron bar of the prison you have become: a longer extension of the cell in which all humans are born, come into screaming. Scream and the high, shrill falsetto voice you never ever want echoes, ripples, and bangs. The jangling keys, the slow drag boot heel, the black scuff marks. You can't see the guard and the guard will not see Juvenile Johnny curved over the bottom bunk like an elegant woman he is not. Stop. But no one will. Stop receding scenarios dubbed over and over and over and over.* There are many unimaginables, and when I try to scream, there is no sound, so I gotta talk to myself to deconstruct myself—and maybe you and us, too. For me, it is survival on so many levels. Coltrane said, *There is never any end.…There are always new sounds to imagine; new feelings to get at. And always, there is the need to keep purifying these feelings and sounds so that we can really see what we've discovered in its pure state.* See, Lxxxx, I'm trying to get to that pure state—pure sound, a way of existing on this place we call earth. I wanna feel brand new all the time.

Picture little Lxxxx, black hair tangled, rubbing her marble eyes, trying to focus on blood trickling down her father's face, trying to understand domestic violence, and all little Lxxxx knows is love. Again, silence is louder than all sound ever created. Consider how we strive for a truth or righteousness in our lives, and when we do find it, it's like we were duped. Red card ain't where the red card supposed to be. Pea not under the middle walnut shell—it never is. Rabbit in the hat a rat. Thinking of a number between one and ten, and it's always twenty-five. We get pulled this way, that way, and for what? I got caught up in your memories and found myself lying in the hospital bed looking up at your mother through your marble eyes, hearing that faint echo—*Is she still a virgin?*—after your attempt to leave this place we call earth. And Lxxxx, I'm trying to break you free from the gizmos and wires. *Wake up!* I'm trying to pry open your lips so you can tell your mother, *Yes, I am pure*. It's like being mute, and the body electrocuted. I could be Baldwin's Sonny in "Sonny's Blues," banging on the piano loud, then really loud, trying to get someone to hear me—to really hear me—yet, nothing. Your body violently shaking, and it's actually me trying to Lazarus you. Then from a tunnel you emerge just on the other side of the light that has been pulling you, only to discover darkness again, and you're fighting now (always was and will be), moving through another tunnel, struggling toward a decibel, a sound, and it's your mother's soft *mi amor*.

I was incarcerated twice, so understand, I feel your pain. The first time, the FBI and Special Task Force had my house under surveillance because of what I had once called a side hustle. According to the FBI's Kingston Files, we were a well-organized crime group with a sophisticated operation of fencing stolen laptop computers. I do not dispute the facts; I admit it was me coming out of an office building in Fairfax County, Virginia, with ten laptops valued at over twenty thousand dollars. When the police had flashed their reds and blues, white Boy from Clifton Terrace had hit the gas, and we almost got away until, coming out of the parking lot, we were side-rammed by an unmarked cruiser. Spinning and spinning, and the car would not stop, and I'm trying to find a way out of the pirouette, to halt the madness. The reds, the blues, and thank God this arrest will not be for the quarter-kilo of narcotic stashed in the safe in my room. It's the difference between eighteen months and a decade. In those eighteen months of confinement, I told myself *never again* only to be released one morning and commit multiple new felony offenses by nightfall. What I am trying to say is, I didn't get it right the first time.

There is something about the streets that stays inside you like a dormant virus—you can't shake it; it lives with you and, in many ways, shapes who you are to become. I don't know if there is a cure, but I do know that one can live with the echo of shots fired, the human mass of bodies choked in stairwells clutching gun handles and crack stems, the dead bodies. We have to turn tragedy into triumph? You could have told me a different narrative, yet this is the one you chose to share, and I consider nothing accidental. When you wrote about being much younger than the rest of your siblings, I knew then that I do not know your complete story. Lxxxx, if your life and my life are intersected by prison, then I am sure this intersection runs deeper than what we both know of being locked up, which is not the central motif of our existence, yet society helps propel this misconception by labeling us CONVICTED for the rest of our lives.

I often talk about my father, whom I consider essential to my maturation as a man in this world. Without him, there is no me. He is my rock, and the memoir I am writing is tentatively titled *Father, Forgive Me.* I will be sending you several peeks from the book. Perhaps in this way you will be able to understand my path to prison and after. I have to write the introduction for next year's issue of *Tidal Basin Review* on the prison industrial complex. Lxxxx, I know that prison is a difficult mandate in that it must represent a physical place where law and order can be administered, yet the administration and maintenance of such a place places a heavy burden on those mandated to "oversee." The elephant in the room is always race, especially when it comes to the disproportionate numbers in terms of demographics within penal institutions. According to the Sentencing Project, "More than 60% of the people in prison are now racial and ethnic minorities. For Black males in their thirties, 1 in every 10 is in prison or jail on any given day." I have seen too much violence and rape on the inside to deny that we need to do better in the rehabilitation process. Sometimes it comes down to just staying alive in prison.

Some questions to consider would be: What does the average person who has never been locked up fail to consider when they side with the death penalty, mandatory sentencing, and the outdated methods prisons use? As the leader of the free world, why is America last to address the idea of incarceration? Perhaps I can use quotes from you while I am working through this intro. The biggest thing is to figure how to enter the essay.

R

JOURNAL NOTE TO [SELF]:
OPEN DOOR——   .

Maple leaves billow up then spiral down; the gray poodle's leash tangles itself around a DO NOT PARK sign; the late model sedan's vibrant echo is bending the corner; the incoming sparrow's zigzagged wingspan teeters, a slug in its beak; the sudden crack of light between clouds, and then darkness; black stilettos dragging the right side of the sidewalk every half-step; off the river into storefront crevices, the wind howls while the radiator clangs and rattles from a first-floor apartment window. They do come and go without thought, without care—the people who summon the block alive. They get-up-go-to-work, pay the landlord (not Peter) while robbing Paul (or any other creditor). Stagnant cumulus clouds represent a truth refusing to shine on faces almost erased. Light is empirical to humans' concept of all-knowing, yet the unknown to the known world participates in a perfunctory ritual with no real vision. They walk in tailored mohair, cashmere, linen, silk, and denim, chained to the labels on their behinds or breastplates, lost in the glitter of image and a universal belief in the eight-hour workday. Success is not a chronological event the long-suffering proletariat will discover too late in time. The city be gray haze, dust dizzied in the breezeway, nomadic hearts moving swiftly. Humans disappear only to emerge from a hole in the ground lined with train track, ultimately (re)appearing at the side door of a building that displays: MEMORY LANE.

EXCERPT I: THE REAL HU

1981 to 1983 —— WASHINGTON, DC

MAIL CALL: LXXXX PXXXX
INMATE NUMBER (37XXXXXX)
FEDERAL DETENTION CENTER
PO BOX 329002
BROOKLYN, NY 11232

THE REAL HOWARD UNIVERSITY, 1981

Imagine a clarion call from a familial glass horn difficult to resist:
a sweet siren. Its tenorpull inescapable, and you've been dragged
under by its metallic wake over and over, methodically, and it is
the most beautiful *hum* within rooms the mind constructs. Rooms
closing themselves off. Internal mechanisms of body and brain are
predicated on sound and, to a lesser extent, a white cloud swirling
uncontrollably through a glass cylinder. Emitting a multifaceted *hum*
switching on and off upon command, igniting a voice. A seductive
slow *hum* informing you you crave what the body no longer harbors.
From the brain, which controls the senses, the mere inhalation of
air replicates what cocaine smells like when ignited at its flashpoint.
Then there is the palate, a medicinal taste, and the body can almost
conjure smoke funneling from pipe to lung. Eardrums play tonal
tricks as the butane lighter's *flick* triggers a photographic hunger:
eyes watching the process by which the lips wrap around a glass stem
and the lungs involuntarily—then voluntarily—suck the sultry flame,
igniting a beige rock as it melts through meshed screens, expanding
the chest with smoke until you are high—higher than the last defunct
star.
    Sophomore year. Second semester on a Wednesday in Locke
Hall. Exiting a classical mythology class, I walked briskly across
campus, taking in the cherry trees that had not yet begun to bloom,
past the outdated football stadium where one could hear a whistle
dictate wind sprints, to Drew Hall where Patrick, from Miami, and
Tony, a native of Whiteville, North Carolina, roomed together on the
second floor. Drew was an all-male dorm facing the football stadium,
and its concrete steps were a stone's throw from McMillian Reservoir

Park, which supplied DC's municipal water. The three of us met freshman year and discovered a connection in our southernness amidst so many students from the North. This day should not have been different than any other where we smoked weed, maybe dropped some orange sunshine, listened to albums spin around a Technics turntable, and of course, talked mad shit—only, when I entered the dorm room, they both asked if I wanted to play baseball.

Consider this: on the way over, I had donned a gray wool scarf around my neck to deflect the cold penetrating my twenty-year-old frame. The comment didn't register or seem logical. Patrick walked over to his wooden desk, opened the drawer, and retrieved a small ball of aluminum foil barely the size of a pinky's fingernail. Tony went to the closet on his side of the room and pulled out a circular glass pipe from the walk-in closet. I would soon discover this was not for smoking marijuana. Patrick simultaneously opened the foil, which revealed a small solid ball.

I was like, "Patrick, where the fuck you get that?" No answer.

For the first time, I detected a difference in both my friends' demeanor. Taking out a razor blade from the top desk drawer, Patrick shaved a small piece of the rock and placed it on top of the stem standing vertical in the glass bowl. He then reached in the bottom drawer and produced a small red butane torch, pulling the lever with his forefinger until gas leaked from the nozzle.

I sat on the bed thinking this hardcore pharmaceutical-type shit might not be for me. Tony pulled a lighter from his pants pocket and flicked its wheel until a blue flame ignited the gaseous odor that morphed into sleek fire. Patrick placed the glass stem protruding from the bowl at an angle to his lips and lit the open-ended vertical stem, its top full of meshed screens to stream the rock once it melted into oil-base.

The smoke began as a tornado swirl until it filled the bowl and had nowhere to escape, stuck in suspended animation. A thick white cloud. As Patrick continued inhaling through the stem, he released his forefinger from the air hole, and the cornered smoke funneled slow-like to an open passage. The seepage crawled up the vertical stem until it filled his mouth, then lungs. When Patrick could no longer inhale, he removed the flame, and released the pipe from his lips, slowly flushing smoke from his nostrils, then mouth. He passed the bowl, and I mimicked his behavior until my lungs, too, filled. I flushed the smoke and waited for the immaculate conception, something—anything. I felt nothing but the need to breathe. Somehow I felt cheated, like there was this big secret being deliberated and everybody knew it but me. Tony repeated the same steps and soared to a place I did not have a passport to enter.

A month later, Patrick asked me to meet him behind the Blackburn Student Center, whose back side faced the reservoir. After that introduction to cocaine weeks earlier, Patrick told me he copped the drugs on Fairmont Street as powder and cooked it up in a vial, and that maybe we could make extra money selling drugs—either weed or cocaine. He brought along Craig Davis, a second-semester freshman from Miami, and we meandered to where the sloping grass provided a clear water view but was blocked from main campus. We lit a joint, and Craig talked about his father, how he worked on the docks in Miami smuggling weed and cocaine from the Bahamas to the states. His father had connections with the Cubans, South Americans, and the Eleutheran Islands.

Craig scoffed at the fast-burning weed, claiming he could score a better grade on the streets in Miami, or the Bottom, as he called his hometown. He promised that if we ponied up our student loan money, we could cop some good weed there and get paid. Although Patrick hailed from Miami, too, it was evident during our conversation that he and Craig had grown up in two different worlds within the same city.

A flock of egrets hovered motionless, suspended in midair over the reservoir, while we sat hillside. Since our first day on campus, we'd watched privileged kids flaunt their parents' brown-paper-bag-and-blue-veined wealth with expensive cars and designer clothes—that Jack and Jill shit we could not be a part of, Jack and Jill being a social society introduced during the 1930s to offer African American children a place to socialize with families on the same economic level. In other words, no single parents, no average income, and no bad credit need apply. Jack and Jill parents were doctors and dentists, and their children dined at expensive restaurants in Adams Morgan and Dupont Circle on monthly allowances.

Patrick and Craig completed the drive to Miami in a weekend.

The knock came at my dorm room door on a Sunday shortly after midnight. Craig entered first and opened a light blue suitcase containing two pounds of some of the prettiest marijuana I'd laid eyes on in my twenty years of living, the odor so pungent it instantly gave me a contact. Patrick, right behind Craig, brought a bottle of cognac from his coat pocket. We smoked and drank whiskey until morning yellow pierced my windowpanes, stabbing sickles of light through the smoke. The next day, money came quick—so quick bank accounts had to be opened because money wrapped in rubber bands under the mattress would not suffice. New friends materialized as if by *abracadabra*. Most students hadn't seen me before because my parents were not on their parents' economic level. These new "friends" appear because you have something they want—need. Drugs render you invincible, narcissistic, arrogant; nonetheless, you mount the crest of the wave you've been given, and you *ride, baby, ride.*

At night I sat alone and fingered through the dollar bills, high off the ink smell. Even if something was slightly off-kilter in my physical presentation, I couldn't see it, couldn't feel the slippage or the torque tugging at my heels, whispering, *slow down, baby boy, slow down.*

Manicured grass and a canopy of maple leaves on campus
transitioned from emerald green to rustic brown, and the short-
sleeve Polo shirts turned into button-down Oxfords and V-neck
argyles. Going into the fall semester, I had developed close
friendships with Janice and Chrissy, whom I met over the summer
while taking classes. Janice, from St. Louis, was short and dark-
skinned, with closely cropped hair. Chrissy was light-skinned with
sandy hair and grew up originally in Pittsburgh and then Bethesda,
Maryland. In 1940, Chrissy would have passed Howard's paper
bag test regarding skin color, while Janice would have enrolled in a
college down south unless her parents had developed connections
amongst the Negro wealthy bourgeoisie. Maybe if her parents had
been doctors, lawyers, or dentists, Janice would have been admitted
for all the uplifting of the race her parents had done.

Since Chrissy lived with her mom in Bethesda instead of
on campus, Janice and I often caught the 70 on Georgia Avenue to
Silver Spring, then transferred to a Ride On to reach Chrissy's house
on weekends and hang out. Part of me wanted a relationship with a
woman, but having felt the stinging loss of a high school lover my
freshman year in college, I kept pretty women at arm's length.

One Thursday at school, Janice and I were hanging at
The Munch Out, decompressing from classes. Many students who
frequented The Munch Out were dubbed "the lunch outs," mainly
because they congregated at the pub all day drinking pints of draft
beer, sometimes firing up weed right in the open. Some were so bold
as to do lines of cocaine on mirrors, all while dressed in designer
gear, talking about how much money their folks got, where they
come from, who they know.

"I wonder what happened to Chrissy. My weekend begins
today, and you know, this place is getting deader by the minute with
all these superficial, fake-ass muthafuckas up in here. Can't believe
she left me hanging today." Janice mentioned this while drowning
in the foam of her last beer. I was tiring of the superficial, fake-ass
muthafuckas, as well, so I asked if she wanted to come over to my
house to hang. "Why not?" she said, and we walked up the stairs,
exiting the student center to where the usual suspects congregated
out front, smoking cigarettes, giving each other dap, trying to be
seen when ain't nobody looking—God's gift to humans on a day
God wasn't giving up a thang. The no-book-carriers dressed to

the nines—hair curled, pressed, a Philly fade, dreadlocks indicating intellectual diarrhea—them folks. We passed the fine arts building, where students practiced dance steps out front in leg-warmers and leotards, preparing for Broadway and the big screen. We passed the world-famous Ira Aldridge Theatre, which had featured a legacy of African American actors such as Owen Dodson, Roxie Roker, Ossie Davis, Lynn Whitfield, Debbie Allen, Phylicia Rashad, and a host of others. All this black history we walked by, buzzed out of our minds.

Grover Washington's saxophone flowed red cabernet out of my ceiling speakers as we smoked a joint and kissed to the light of a yellow caution blinking in our heads. The only glow in the room came from the television's static emitting a white screen of snowflakes. I wanted to retreat from what I knew surely to be a mistake, but I could not, and we kissed long and intense until our bodies warmed a gorgeous rage. We disrobed while lips probed cheekbones, behind the ear, the chin, becoming familiar lovers under the sheets, tracing circles, pantomiming emotions tossed side to side hung inside midnight's quarter moon. Clockwise, then counterclockwise, our hands held each other's fate. We were too afraid to exhale, that the moment would be lost. Our bodies collided, and we collapsed into each other's heavy breathing and slept until dawn, never to repeat the act with each other again.

Craig dragged the rustic footlocker from the makeshift bedroom next to the bar in the basement of the single-family home he rented uptown. He unlatched the gold metal locks, and our eyes met one hundred pounds of Columbian Red—the most I had ever seen. The weed was packed stack upon stack in Ziploc bags. If that didn't surprise Patrick, Tony, and me enough, Jesse, from Bartow, Florida, who had befriended Craig a few months back and was now officially part of our crew, said, "but check this, fellas," and tossed five sticks of black opium on the bar beside the hashish. Each stick weighed approximately twenty-eight grams and bore the stamped imprint MADE IN INDIA in bold block lettering.

The fact that Jesse was from Florida and perhaps the most vocal and demonstrative of us all lent an even greater mystique to our presence on campus. His connection with hashish brought us together, and we found our southernness to be a collective strength. We were trying to become a family.

Craig reached under the bar and placed a solid one-pound brick of brown hash on top of the weed. He reached under the bar again and a mirror full of the white powder we had come to love appeared. Up until this point, we had only been selling weed and doing coke recreationally, but we knew that would soon change. Craig assured us that one day soon, he would be dealing blow this quality or greater, that he was working on a way to smuggle it out of the Eleutheran Islands. All five of us sat at the bar and snorted lines with a rolled-up hundred-dollar bill. I knew this was Grade A product by the way my nose went numb and how the numbness spread throughout my face until it was immobile, and as it began seeping through to my throat, my mind zoomed outside my body to somewhere unrecognizable. White powder offered me psychological transportation to places I'd never been, but more than that, gave me a power beyond what I could give myself, and I knew that everyone at the bar felt the same.

The weed was not as potent as from previous Miami trips, but definitely potent enough to sell to the average consumer. Now that I lived off campus, my mainline to students went through the athletic dorm, Cook Hall, and Cat Daddy, my homeboy from Montgomery, Alabama, who played on the football team. It wasn't until I fronted him a couple of pounds weeks later—along with opium and hash—that he concocted a creative plan to sell a gram of the opium or hash with a dime bag for seven dollars. He revealed this intricate scheme when I came to collect money one Sunday evening. The smell of sweet fried corn, macaroni and cheese, smothered pork chops, and cornbread prompted me to ask for a plate when I arrived. After dinner, we discussed business. Cat Daddy enjoyed a different clientele than I did. By living on campus, he had direct access to an entire student body.

"The way I see it, Hook, we can give 'em this special and they'll think they getting something for free." My closest friends now called me Hook because of the way I could put together a drug deal and seduce people to invest money in large packages of marijuana. In other words, I could hook 'em and sell a dream. "They can lace the weed with hash or opium or smoke it by itself—either way, they getting high and coming back, homeboy. They'll love anything I put down, cause you know all I gotta do is cosign the product, and I can move all the drugs you got. And that's no bullshit."

I had to admit Cat Daddy made sense. Broken down, we received the weed at a hundred dollars a pound. Even at that rate, we could make two thousand dollars with overly large sacks. We wouldn't make as much on the opium and hash, but it would boost the weed sales.

Meanwhile, to my parents, I woke up every day jostling to class, jotting notes, and dashing to the stacks to study until the clock tower struck two in the morning. This was the verbal contract my parents thought was agreed upon. The phone calls turned into lies upon lies. *Of course, I studied out of my mind, and yes, I would be graduating in four years.* I masked my secret life by being far away from home, out of the reach of eyes that could snap me back to rationality in an instant. There was never a consideration of what they would think. Point blank: I didn't give a damn.

One Friday during the middle of the fall semester, Patrick, Tony, and I caught the bus back over to Craig's to talk business, and he informed us that one of his connections from Miami would be arriving in a few days to front him a brick—approximately one thousand grams. At that level, the coke "usually" hasn't been stepped on with a cut of mannitol to stretch the gram quantity. With all this good news, I still worried about cash flow. Although we sold a lot of weed, the money never added up like I thought it would.

I came to learn in this game, you spread money around, especially when people work for you. The dealers who worked for me developed problems only money could solve: they had to deal with customers coming with short money; they had to front people to get them hooked, to develop relationships; they had to pay bills and eat. Because they were dependent on me, I subscribed to the illusion of power, even if it required losing money. When the shipment arrived, Craig fronted us two ounces and we transitioned from recreational users to cocaine suppliers.

The three of us had a lot to learn about powder. Our first step in this process began with going to a drug paraphernalia store on 20th and R Streets near Dupont Circle. We bought a sifter, snow seals to package the powder, an Ohaus triple-beam scale, a bottle of mannitol, meshed screens, a vial, and a freebase pipe, and then returned home. Mannitol was the most important purchase, as it would be used to stretch the powder into more grams. Before cutting the powder, there needed to be some type of gauge as to the drug's strength or potency. This was found by measuring out a gram of powder and cooking it into freebase. While the water was boiling, Patrick measured out the drug on the Ohaus scale, added .3 grams of baking soda, inserting the mixed concoction into the glass vial, and then used a spoon to scoop enough water to fill the vial half full. He placed the vial into the boiling water and let the cocaine cook for a good minute. Because we didn't speak, the only sound in the kitchen emanated from the rattling vial in the pot, the clearing of throats, and heavy breathing. All four of us sweated, our eager eyes locked in on the vial.

After a minute, Patrick reached inside the pot, grabbed the vial by its black cap with a dishrag, shielding his fingers from the heat, and twisted it off. White steam rose up, emitting a strong medicinal odor. He scooped more boiling water from the pot and

25

slowly added a drop or two. Patrick raised the vial to the kitchen light and flicked the side with his middle finger, slowly turning the glass cylinder. Around and around, and as if by magic—droplets of oil descended from the murky water to the bottom of the vial to join in a beige mass. Patrick swirled the oil in a circular motion and the beige mass became a rock. He rolled the base out of the vial like he was throwing dice against the curb. We stared at it like it was holy.

"How much you think it weigh?" Tony whispered.

"I dunno," Patrick mumbled, shaking his head.

"Put it on the scale and check it out," I said as I grabbed the scale and calibrated it to zero.

The newly formed rock placed on the scale balanced at .9 grams, making it ninety percent pure. However, to be certain, we put the drug to the test by freebasing. One of the customary acts of freebasing was to allow the person who cooked the rock to go first. Patrick attached a cotton ball to the end of a hanger wire, dipped it into a glass full of grain alcohol, and I lit the soaked cotton with a lighter. He sizzled the base rock with the torch, sucking the glass stem of the pipe hard, and after he pulled the wire hanger away, his eyes shone star-bright, confirming the drug's potency. Then Tony and I smoked our samples.

Unlike that first time back in Drew Hall when I thought basing was a waste of time, I immediately heard *bells*, and then a *siren*, followed by a slow, seductive *hum* speaking *love* to my inner conscious, the rush funneling through me like a runaway cyclone. Tony experienced the same furious ride as we nodded our heads in concurrence. With ninety percent cocaine, we could place a "half cut" and stretch the blow. That meant for every ounce, we added half an ounce of mannitol. We went to work that night bagging 25s, 50s, and grams in snow seals. The ounces cost fifteen hundred dollars, and we could profit two thousand on each. The only thing we hadn't counted on was the amount of work one had to put into selling large amounts of cocaine. We basically needed to develop a clientele on the yard, giving samples away to convince people we had high-quality blow and get new users hooked. On the other hand, Craig and Jesse dealt mostly off campus in the city and engaged with a seedier clientele whose motto was cash and carry—but their distribution base larger. They made friends with street people—pimps and prostitutes. Jesse befriended Whip, Radar, and Big Stew, who lived together across the street from Howard on Georgia Avenue. Whip and Radar did not attend school and worked odd jobs to help Big Stew—a junior who hailed from Wilson, North Carolina—with the rent. Their apartment offered easy access for students on campus and became Jesse's base of operations, whereas Craig often remained a mystery in terms of his dealings.

The semester ended with neither Patrick, Tony, nor I making much money, because we tried to maintain the illusion of being big-time drug dealers, spending money hand over fist even though the money never added up. We also ingested entirely too much coke, both snorting and freebasing. A couple times, we went overboard and smoked all our supply in one night and had to funnel money from our marijuana sales to cover the coke tab with Craig.

Our little college empire really started crumbling when Tony got arrested jumping the turnstile in the subway. A half-ounce of powder in his possession, and he wouldn't pay seventy cents for a train ride. We were over at Craig's house freebasing at the bar. Jesse inhaled a big blast of cocaine smoke and fell slap-out on the floor. The collect call brought everybody's high down to nothing. Craig drove to the DC jail where they were detaining Tony and bonded him out. With Tony facing a felony conviction and supervised probation, he concluded the drug game might not be for him.

I never thought about going to jail. It literally never crossed my mind.

MOVE TO HARVARD STREET, 1983

Four continuous weeks after Christmas break, I stayed clear of cocaine because of what happened to Tony, until one night in Wheaton, Maryland. Patrick was in the kitchen sampling a package Craig had dropped off to us to sell. I declined, but Patrick refused to give up on making money, so he accepted. By now Tony had moved back on campus, hoping to realign himself with his pursuit of a degree in chemical engineering. Wanting to follow Tony's lead, I sat on the couch in the adjacent living room working statistical problems, trying to understand standard deviations and remain true to my promise of intense focus when it came to the books so I could graduate with a degree in economics; however, the gravitational pull from the medicinal smell emitted from the kitchen became too much. The high, in its beautiful contradiction, called to me lovingly. I longed to hear its synthetic voice, so I walked against my will into the kitchen, picked up the clouded bowl when handed to me, pulled hard, and the *bells* rang once again, and keep on ringing, sucking me back up into the life I wanted to abandon.

No matter how hard we tried, Patrick and I still couldn't turn a profit because we spent too much time in the kitchen listening to the clattering of that glass vial. Some months, our situation got so bad we juggled the rent money to pay off our debt, only to get another package and fall further in debt. Craig wasn't pressuring us, but he did want his money, and we felt obligated to pay. Although we were friends, business was business. By the end of the semester, we had lost the house because we weren't paying rent on time.

In June, the two of us moved to a row house one block from Howard on Georgia and Harvard Street. The neighborhood, like so many near Howard's campus, was run-down and infested with drugs. The first week we moved in, from our front steps, we watched a bedraggled man run out of the adjacent alley, bent low, nothing but asshole and elbows, chased by another man on crutches with a baseball bat in hand. Evidently, right behind our rented row house, they sold Love Boat, which is formaldehyde pressured-cooked with propane gas. You could either dip a cigarette into the liquid, which was called a Sherm Stick, or spray it onto marijuana, producing the stronger mixture of Love Boat.

A junior from Philly we called King Freak managed the house and found students on campus to rent rooms. Patrick got the basement because he could pay a little more, and I rented the front room on the first floor, which really wasn't a room at all; however, I fixed it up with bamboo blinds and bedsheets for privacy. I didn't dig the crude setup, but we needed to move fast, and King Freak had the place. Cat Daddy ended up subleasing an upstairs room for the summer instead of staying in the dorm. My partnership with him lasted a few months, but slowly fizzled as he relied more and more on a New York City connection. Where cocaine had once been a fad, it was now prevalent throughout the city, the nation. Richard Pryor torched himself freebasing. There were rumors about Chaka Khan, Natalie Cole, even Gil Scott-Heron, one of the most political and socially conscious artists of my generation who sang about the perils of angel dust. A nation crawling on all fours searching for cocaine crumbs that might have spilled while smoking.

The novelty of being the only students on campus with the drug was dying. Just by my association with Miami and Craig, I kept a little juice. However, if I'd paid attention in Principles of Economics I, I would have probably learned about the dynamics of supply and demand and understood that, as my total output decreased, my total input increased, thereby always creating a deficit. But I skipped class most of the time and got a C.

Shortly after the move, I secured a part-time job conducting political surveys over the phone at the Thomas Hilton Research Firm. I called random people and asked their opinions on issues before legislation in the House or Senate. This was when I began noticing the duality of DC in terms of neighborhoods and economics. I worked four days a week uptown on Connecticut Avenue, where businesses thrived amongst a bustling and bright community of well-kept townhouses, apartments, and small boutiques—mostly cottage industry stuff. Then I returned to Harvard Street right in the middle of economic deprivation and mayhem to be reminded that life is an everyday struggle, that everyone ain't on a level playing field. Perhaps these neighborhoods were trying to recover from the riots of the '60s, when Martin and Malcolm were gunned down, and the blood-red rage of Black America wanted to burn something to the ground. Only thing—they burned their own neighborhoods.

For the first time, I could gauge the internal pulse of Northwest DC outside the insulated college experience. On humid summer nights, Cat Daddy, Patrick, and I sat on the front stoop soaking up the corner's lamplight with our not-yet-twenty-one-faces, and shot rats coming out of the alley with a pellet gun. The pellets bounced off their pelts, sending each verminous creature squealing behind the green dumpster. And there were the voices of the city: windows opening and closing, a couple in the upstairs bedroom arguing about the light bill, children riding silver-spoke bicycles up and down the cracked sidewalks. More than that, cars blasting stereos with go-go, the indigenous music of the city based on call and response, provided the only soundtrack we needed as we self-medicated with weed late into the night.

I often noticed a young, slender woman walking by our house to the one she stayed in five doors down. One evening after work, I sat by myself drinking a can of beer on the stoop when the woman came down the street. I spoke like I'd always done, except this time I let it be known I wanted her to stop and talk. "Hey, what up," I said. "How you doing today?"

She couldn't have been much older than me. She wasn't in college, but I didn't know what she did for a living.

"I'm cool. I walked to the store to get something to drink. It's kinda hot in my place." She had a bottle wrapped tight in a brown bag. Old English or Colt 45, I thought to myself.

She surprised me with, "You wanna party a little bit? I know you got weed. I see you and your boys out here smoking sometime."

"Hook," I said, getting off the steps.

Her name was Olivia and she stayed in a converted rooming house. There was a kitchen. No living or dining room, just a succession of doors on each floor. We walked upstairs to her room on the third floor. She opened the door to a crib in the corner with a baby not more than a year old inside. The baby started hollering, and I remember thinking maybe this wasn't where I needed to be.

"Here, drink some of this beer and light up one of them joints you got, Hook."

Olivia gave the baby a pacifier. After the child fell asleep and we were high, we had mechanical sex—the kind of sex you initiate because that's what a man and a woman are supposed to do when they're together, at least that's what I was taught from the older boys in my old neighborhood back in Birmingham, Alabama.

When I went back to visit her, she'd vanished, never to be seen again. All I thought about was her lugging an infant around DC. What if that were my mother, and I was that little child in the crib? I resolved to be a better student when school started back up.

In the next few months, life rattled me around like a runaway locomotive—fast and furiously hard. Since my job at Thomas Hilton was only part time, I eventually fell behind in rent because I didn't want to supplement my income selling drugs. I had refused the offer of an ounce on consignment from Cat Daddy, knowing if I started smoking coke again, I might not bounce back. Patrick had secured a full-time moving job and was able to help pay. Even he came to realize this cocaine game broke you down five ways from Sunday.

Although I had promised to stay clear of cocaine, I went to King Freak with a proposition, convincing him to invest in the drug game. This would help pay rent and tuition for the upcoming fall. If people wanted to get something for nothing, I could sell them a bag full of dreams in their pursuit of greed.

December 1983. Cold is a dreadful thing. Say I hop the turnstile
with two dollars in my pocket. There is an art to busying oneself to
pass time: in the back corner of the last subway car from DC to the
outskirts of Northern Virginia, then back over the Potomac River
into a subway hole where I want the end of time to eat me alive. Say
the sky is falling or fell yesterday. Nowhere to run, and options do
not exist when flashing red lights produce a siren inside your head.
Here is where the narrative clutters—events entering and exiting
swift. The fall hard and in four/four time, the metal slide off a five-
string guitar echoing in your ear. A sudden fool's melody lifts you up,
and then a downdraft of B-flats escorts you closer to the blues. One
decision after another, disastrous insomuch as dreams are not real—
as in, everything's a magician's trick where I will never guess which
hand the silver coin is in, yet I try; yet I fail.

Addiction grabs the body, everything zooming at the speed
of sound threaded through a needle's head. Freebase amplifying that
sound, louder and louder, incorrigible. Two women in an apartment
performing sexual acrobatics on me, to each other—we all in. Sweat
dripping down the bridge of my nose onto the mirror, one droplet
at a time. The rock is holy. Stark-naked females dance seductively
inside the mirror's reflection. Cage the outside world, along with its
problems: place pebble in stem. Sizzle then… *last one. Last one. The
Last One.* Believe this lie, if only for a moment. It is never the *last.*
Man's weakness hangs between his legs. *Come on in, baby. Have a seat.
Let me take your coat, boo. Jesse got a fine friend. He sent you, huh? Lucky
us! What you need to drink? We got cognac. Wanna smoke before you go?
You don't need nothing. Let's take it to the bedroom. What your name again,
suga?* Open the snow seal. *Last one. Last one. The Last One.* Mix with
baking soda. Hear the vial rattling product along with the brain—
around and around. Place pebble in stem. Sizzle then fall into a ravine
alongside the seductive bodies. All night, fantasies fulfilled—the only
requirement: make the beige pebble appear then disappear. What's
yours is theirs in a matter of hours.

We smoked until not even the crumbs were left, because *the
rock is holy.* Say I walked inside a swarm of noontime pedestrians
unaware of the locality of the living. In order to end you have to
begin, and I was between going and stop. I could not tell you if birds
pipe strange trajectories or if the wind howls when the sun is a full
orb. Say the clothes on my body were on my body yesterday and the

day before. I could not tell you the time of day or the month, because time and space were inconsequential. Routines terrible the mind. When you do nothing but poison the body, every day becomes a test to see how close to the threshold of death you can venture before receding back.

Every wrong decision and deal culminated with seeking refuge in Tony's dorm room while he traveled to Whiteville for Christmas break, because there was nowhere in the city to call home when King Freak kicked me out, threatening bodily harm if I did not pay his investment money back. I crashed briefly with Jesse and his girlfriend in their studio apartment on 16th Street, but pride made me leave after a week because I didn't want to tell him two women seduced me into smoking my entire supply in one night. I wandered aimlessly for days, sleeping anywhere I could: a closet, a hallway, a car, the train, and finally, Tony's room.

There were no brakes to slow down the collision with catastrophe, so I sped up full speed, preparing for the inevitable train wreck. Hidden in a darkened room for two days straight, I could not hear Christmas bells jingling nor distant carols sung. No holiday cheer for the addict tucked inside a room in the fetal position, trying to sleep away the wretchedness and the uncertainty. On the third day of self-reflection, I gathered the courage to call my parents and humbly ask for a bus ticket home—for good. The city had eaten its young and spit its cartilage out onto the hard carcass of the streets.

Four months after returning home, I received a phone call from Cat Daddy, first forgiving me for running off with his package, then reporting that Whip and Radar had fired seven bullets at point-blank range into Jesse's skull with a .357 Magnum. Evidently that hadn't been enough, because when Jesse's girlfriend discovered the body coming home from her swing shift, she found his six-foot frame submerged in the bathtub, electrocuted by a plugged-up iron thrown into the bloody water.

The violent death prompted Craig's move back to Miami. Patrick and Tony returned to school, leaving the drug game behind. And here—here is where my narrative begins.

3

CONNECTIONS AND DISCONNECTIONS

I received the books—*The Genealogy of Morals* and the dictionary/thesaurus you sent—as well your excerpt. I managed to read about twenty pages, and I can see how you got sucked into the drug game. Money is everybody's mistress, yet this part of the drug game is something I cannot relate to because I didn't come up smoking crack. But I can relate to chasing a dream. We all do that, one way or another. I always wondered what went on at Howard. I never learned much about black colleges growing up in the Bronx. Sounds like a lot of classism to me, that whole W.E.B. Dubois double-consciousness debate playing out among students. I wonder if your painter friend Margaret Bowland can capture that with a brush?

On Monday, I finished reading *Paula* by Isabel Allende. It's a memoir written in epistle form to her daughter, who became ill, fell into a coma, and never woke up. She died within a year. The story travels back and forth through time as Allende explains the history of their family and the political ties they had in Chile after it was taken over by the military coup. I believe it's the best book Allende has ever written. She has also written *The House of the Spirits, Eva Luna,* and a few other works of fiction. However, I am much fonder of this biography because it shows how she developed the ideas to write these books. *Paula* shows the journey of the writer and provides an inside look on how stories are created. It's a very spiritual and enlightening piece of work. You should definitely read it when you have some downtime.

Allende says something interesting that has stayed with me. She was teaching a writing class at a university in California and did not know how to make the class interesting and worthwhile. She decided to tell the students to write a bad book, an awful piece of writing. This allowed the students the freedom to let their thoughts flow without focusing on errors. The students edited throughout the course, and by the end, one of them even got published. Any writer can write a bad story—the objective is to get the story out, and I agree with that concept.

Allende also mentions how novels are born beyond the thought process, that there is a deeper connection with the Divine that ordains stories to come to life on paper. She would save newspaper articles of tragedies for years at a time without understanding why. Eventually, she used those clippings to support the ideas and characters in her stories. Every writer has a greater purpose to serve. Allende said that people would often tell her their life stories. She would eventually use these stories as characters in her books. Randall, we all go through things in life, and there are stories to be told everywhere.

I also discovered *Don Quixote* was written by a Miguel de Cervantes while he was in prison—very interesting! Sharing your story with me lets me know almost anything can be overcome. I want to take that leap of faith you took; I want to believe in my dreams and myself, and you are helping me. I spoke to my lawyer, and things are still up in the air, but I'm learning how to make the most of my time.

I have been wrapped up in Luis Rodriguez's memoir, *Always Running*, too. It is phenomenal, and I can't believe I've never heard of it before. Rodriguez moves swiftly through the pages. I never considered any writer a graceful gangster, but he earned that title for sure. I'm going to get into *The Genealogy of Morals* soon because I'm eager to see the "parallelisms regarding the fallacy of color and on skin construction," as you put it. It's interesting how Rodriguez touches on race issues, but really focuses on class struggle and how we—meaning all of us (people of color)—deal with being the underdogs in America. But these issues always make me wonder about America's majority. I mean the white America no one dialogues on, the one Dorothy Allison depicted in *Bastard Out of Carolina*. Class struggle should be an issue involving all of us who live below the invisible medium. These labels and divisions and subdivisions only further cloud the real issues. These problems are older than both of us put together. So, how can literature tackle these issues? How do we touch the average person who doesn't care to read books because they are too busy trying to work and survive? How can short stories address serious issues without losing significance? That's why I liked *The House on Mango Street* so much, because Sandra Cisneros managed to do that with vignettes.

I think I was drawn to you as a friend because we shared a common difference that not too many people in the writing center at SUNY Albany understood. It was our secret, our past, and we were the only two people of color. I was cool with the other folks, but it wasn't the same. I felt connected because we spoke the same language. I loved how you didn't try to assimilate; you wore your difference and celebrated it. Those people in the writing center were all blown away by your swag. You really impressed me, and still do. You are doing everything I dreamed of doing—you made it happen.

Having tunnel vision only helped speed your progress and get you closer to your goals. Nothing and no one got in your way. I couldn't do that—I stumbled and fell, and now I'm back at square one. The funny thing is, it wasn't that I wasn't smart enough. I just couldn't let go of the dumb shit like you did. I felt drawn to the "life," compelled to straddle two worlds because only then did I feel normal. If I gave either side a hundred percent, I always found myself feeling displaced. Does that make any sense? You always make me think, and I love you for it.

I finally got a chance to read Nietzsche. Although the first half is interesting, I jumped to the second, and I'm amazed at how easily this guy confuses me. I love it because he takes reading and interpretation to another level. Nietzsche makes me question the morals imposed by Christianity, society, and the difference between the moral values throughout the Americas—you know: white America and Latin America (Central and South), and the Caribbean, as well, in contrast with Europe and the rest of the Christian world. I've never been more certain of my own curiosities, and now the questions I've been pondering make a lot more sense. Everything I have read throughout this period of my life has led to the same question: what is Man's search for meaning and life's purpose which is guided by the Divine? It is amazing how even mistakes can help map and shape who we are and who we are destined to become. Randall, each of us has a mission that we are uncertain of. How often do we really get to understand and know our true "selves"?

I know I kind of rushed that letter about my past and said a lot, but didn't explain much. Those things are kind of hard to talk about, but I'm trying to get them out. I've been waiting for a reason to write about for years. Actually, I've never been able to write about my suicide attempt, and twenty years later, I'm telling you. I don't feel so vulnerable now that you are sharing your story with me. You got me all in now. Send more when you can. Thank you for helping me find my voice again, for bringing the darkness out—it's helping me heal, and somehow your story is shining a light on the past and helping me see things clearly now. I'm figuring out answers to questions I didn't even understand back then. Tonight I finished the excerpt. I'm sorry about Jesse. That's gotta be some hard shit to deal with.

Lxxxx

4

PROCESS AND ENDING POINT

Interesting point you make about Isabel Allende and the writing process. Purging to break free of constraints. I like that and agree. But when I consider the writing process, I tend to start with the poet Etheridge Knight, who contemplated the relationship between reader and audience as a sacred phenomenon, an unexplained parallel universe of equal exchange, a state of being. The idea of trust between writer and reader is not rooted in, *am I telling you a lie, or am I telling you the truth,* but more based on the idea, *do I trust my reader?* I tend to think writers should be able to lead the reader to a particular subject or "intent" without the reader being aware that's what the writer is doing. Beginning writers all too often make these assumptions about imagery in terms of presentation.

For example, lets look at the following sentence: "I can hear salsa music around the corner." Lxxxx, can we say the writer doesn't trust her reader? The line is presented in a way that leads the reader too much. There is no surprise. No experience. How can we pull the reader through the music? An alternative would be: "A compilation of son montuno, guaracha, chachachá, mambo, y bolero seeped around the corner, spreading electric energy throughout the block." If we embrace this approach, then perhaps more is gained out of the description, presenting the sentence in a way as to make it an experience through imagery while staying true to cultural intent. Another example would be, "I see her in a red dress walking the dog down the street." Again, the writer makes it too easy. This is supposed to be a shared relationship, yet, the writer does not provide a more rounded scene. What if the writer wrote: "The black-and-white dog, walked by a silver-haired woman in a red dress, tows her owner. Each day, the old lady walks the small dog down the street, perhaps reliving summer days when she stopped traffic in her leather miniskirts."

In a previous letter, you also asked, "How can short stories address serious issues without losing significance?" One of the ways would be in themes that convey *choice* and *calling*, as suggested in one of your letters, because of our society's fundamental belief in a free society. The reason I say this is because some people's choices have been geared toward suppressing other people's choices and voices (check Marxism), so to choose a unique path in life—or literature—is revolutionary in our mimetic society. Each person, including you or I, has to be his or her own protagonist, and yes, I am echoing Ralph

Ellison's *Invisible Man*. Remember how the protagonist moved to other people's choices before making his own? Failure doesn't mean we are not capable narrators of life's journey; in failure resides future triumph, yours and mine—bottom line. We have been writing (acting out) stories all our lives, and we conjure those stories through memory; however, that cannot be enough for the writer. Application develops imagination.

Lxxxx, the best advice I ever received from another writer was, "fall in love with someone else's writing before you fall in love with your own," and since you mentioned Isabel Allende and her writing class, let us turn to *The Flagellants* by Carlene Hatcher Polite to further explore the writing life. This book can be viewed as a microcosm of the Black Arts Movement insomuch as Polite deconstructs male and female assumed roles according to the unofficial doctrine of the '60s. Jimson is a virile black male, a poet and an idealist, but fallible, which comes out in his interactions with Ideal, a woman who refuses to subscribe to the tenets around the movement because she believes them to be oppressive. Jimson's flaws reside in his inability to see this woman as equal, oppressing her while he battles the oppressor through revolutionary rhetoric.

Here, I want to use the analogy of music for writing, and the discipline needed for both. Ideal retells the story of Booker Shad, an aspirant musician who thought he was ready to play jazz until he sat in one night with Charlie "Bird" Parker. Bird tells him, "You could develop into a real beautiful cat; but, man, you have got to study….If you really want to play, to become a pro, you will have to step on out, man, and take that step which will not leave you hung up in a room somewhere listening to yourself blow."

Now, if I had to translate this in a way to correspond to the writing journey, it would begin with: *One can be a stunning writer, but one must understand the lineage, those who came before. Know their work in your sleep, and write every day. Step past that which makes you comfortable. Don't fall in love with yourself reciting words into a mirror.*

See, there is really no difference between life and language. Miles and Coltrane knew how to intersect both into a neoteric way of looking in to get that field holla out—sometimes with china white and tap water flamed in a bottle top and soaked up with a cigarette filter, then a syringe. The solution redistributed into the blood stream, bringing euphoria to the body, which is why Miles and Coltrane slow-ground the melody, saturated sound into a KIND OF BLUE. Lxxxx, in order to begin, you have to reach an end point. It is not a matter of being smart enough, as you say. The bottom tip of the rope is where you have to dangle—perhaps your last bit of hope, so you have no choice but to climb back through the hole in which you've fallen. This is what I had to accomplish, because I did not want to let go. I desired to live, as I know you do—if nothing else, for your son. Solitary time will force you to know yourself, as I was forced. There are no easy answers or solutions to difficult problems, especially the ones you face with this court system.

Lxxxx, today the sun is echoing last summer's heat, presenting a future soon to come. A cluster of sparrows outside my windowsill sing of spring. The trees are decorated green. Although the sky hints at blue, it is more gray, reminding us that this world is not a monotone drone. There has been a silence in your life, which is really the universe's way of saying, *I am preparing you for the noise you will make.* Linger in the silence, and use that to be baptized into the living.

Whenever I need to think scenarios through, I often walk the two blocks over to Harlem West Piers and stare blankly at the dark blue Hudson while sitting on one of the three benches facing west. There is something meditative about the movement of liquid, about the wake left by sputtering motorboats, how the receding foam gently brushes against your eardrums like a soft echo. Perhaps it borders on the spiritual in the way egrets glide low, hung inside the glow of a noon sun, and then, without a moment's notice, catch a wind gust at a 90-degree angle. I have this theory about water and how it retains memory through invisible particles floating in the liquid.

Since I claim water as a muse, an entryway into writing, I am preparing a trip to Eleuthera, and more specifically Hatchet Bay. If you remember, I mention Eleuthera in the manuscript. I haven't been back in almost ten years. So please excuse the shortness of this letter, as I have been multitasking these past couple of days. Wanted to get something in the mail before I leave this weekend. I am receiving research money from my school to travel and continue working on my memoir and a few travel essays. I want to get a feel for the landscape, the places and foliage I refused to "see" when I first set foot on the island. Perhaps I can add more detail to my memory. You should be getting the next section soon. Lxxxx, I am still your eyes, yet I refuse to give you redundancy of language, to recycle our conversations as cliché. I promise, I will take you with me.

R

JOURNAL NOTE TO [SELF]:

LOOK SEE

Off the Hudson's riverbank, a walkway runs parallel all the way downtown where buildings sprout from the recesses of earth, trying to be cloud-bound. On the CHERRY WALK there are two lanes: one for spinning bicycle spokes, the other pedestrian-friendly. One hundred yards out from the bank, a small tanker idles, seagulls hanging approximately one hundred yards above its hull. In the backdrop, off to the right side of the walkway, the GEORGE WASHINGTON BRIDGE—that link between two states, a necessary connector—looms, plumb level with cars inching across before the impending rush hour. The wall on the left side of the walkway offers indented images mimicking those gulls that hover a hundred yards out. The gulls cemented in various poses of flight present the ultimate symbol of freedom, suspended. Before the yellow YIELD sign appears, a large billboard asks: HAVE YOU SEEN THE DARK?

EXCERPT II: SLIPPIN' INTO DARKNESS

1984 TO 1990 —— MICHIGAN, BAHAMAS & FLORIDA

MAIL CALL: LXXXX PXXXX
INMATE NUMBER (37XXXXXX)
FEDERAL DETENTION CENTER
PO BOX 329002
BROOKLYN, NY 11232

DESTINY AND FATE, 1984

In late January, two months after Jesse's death execution-style, I was on a Greyhound headed toward Lansing, Michigan. I could no longer reside inside the same house as my parents, who possessed no physical blueprint for how to deal with addiction. There had never been an addict in the family, and the lying and erratic behavior became too overwhelming. My parents did not understand how a drug makes a person callous and self-centered. It was a complicated dilemma. On one hand you had the parents who—due to the mere fact that they had given birth to you, that you came from the same blood—wanted to do anything humanly possible to stop the nightmare inside your head. On the other hand, you had the parents who, in order to save a son, had to release him into this unforgiving world, let him trip, fall, stumble, and damn near die to be reborn again.

Everything had begun to unravel when my unpredictable behavior superseded my ability to become profitable. While back home, instead of getting my life together, I devised intricate schemes to hook people into investing large sums of money in drugs I purchased from Craig in Miami. There was the promise of a big payday. Everybody wants something for nothing; we are conditioned to work hard for what we want when, in reality, we do not want to work hard at all. These investors were upwardly mobile professionals whose lives were already semi-comfortable, yet society told them they needed more—that more was equivalent to success—so these people put money in my hands based on whatever dream I sold them. There were also men of the cloth who gave me investment money, and I

49

am talking about misogynistic storefront preachers who pimped women and smoked and drank like it was legal under the Lord's eyes. Reverend Greene was one of these preachers, standing in the pulpit on Sunday, working the congregation into a fervor, representing a God that just might send him below Hell: in the name of the Father, the Son, and the Holy Spirit, gold tooth and all. This manipulation allowed me to spend money I didn't have, which created a system where I was always dependent on the next investor—until I became careless and spent more than I could replace, thereby owing way too many people.

Because of this debt, I found and wrote a blank check that emptied my father's bank account of more than twenty-five hundred dollars to finance one of my drug-running escapades to Miami. It was during the Christmas holidays, and my father found out before I could replace the money. On a Monday, my father, mother, and sister entered the house through the basement from a day of shopping, and I could tell by their facial expressions that they had been by the bank. The women stared at me lying on the couch as my father ran upstairs and came barreling back down, promptly placing a .38 snubnose to the temple of my head. Emphatically, he cursed and yelled, calling me every kind of muthafucka he could think of. Over and over he kept asking, *Why, Randall? Why, Randall?* How could I steal from my family?

Unable to answer, I remained silent. I wanted my heart to stop beating, but it would not. I wanted to suck the life out of my body until I was nothing, but sadly, I could not. I kept right on living. I turned to my mother, whose smearing mascara seemed to be begging my father not to pull the trigger, not to shoot her only son. My sister, who idolized me as the older brother, covered her eyes. All she could do was cry and yell, *Daddy, no!*

Came home two weeks later after an all-night coke binge, and the bags were packed. *Nigga, you gotta get the hell out of here,* my father asserted. I stepped off the bus thinking Lansing might help clear my head, get my thoughts together, and perhaps be the impetus for a new beginning. My cousin Todd picked me up and drove me to the place I would call home for the next few months. His apartment was small, but two bedrooms and two baths plus a deck wasn't bad for a bachelor.

Staying with someone is a difficult proposition when you are not contributing to the well-being of the household. Bills needed to be paid each week, and the ultimate goal was to pull your body mass up over the proverbial hump—that imaginary object that appeared every Wednesday—and propel that same body mass into Friday to ride that eagle. The eagle needed to fly, someway, somehow, so I began the process of looking for employment under Lansing's gray sky just before February. Mornings be cold as a bitch in the North— witch-tit cold. Everybody gotta get up in the morning, even the soup- hound under the bed. Bring a bone home or something. The daily routine became: walk to the corner, plop a quarter in the slot, pull the door open, grab the paper, come back home, make job calls, circling and x-ing out information. Then out again into the unforgiving hawk—not to be confused with the eagle, and because it's always unforgiving—which ain't happening, at least not yet. On and off city buses. Struggling, all the harder because you're living with someone who is not.

There were more relatives: Todd's sisters, Shayla and Diane, cousins who had fled the Motor City along with their brother, hoping to escape the violence. We were kinfolk, but I didn't know them from a can of spray paint. Family can be strange. My daddy had told me that once, and now I understood what he meant. I would go over to their houses and spend time with them playing cards or talking current events, but I felt like an outsider. They were not my immediate family and didn't care if I got my act together or not. What I did know of my cousins is that they liked to have a good time. Soon cocaine was on a mirror, the folded funnel of a dollar bill placed in my hands, and then I was home once again.

Todd put me out of his house unexpectedly in the middle of winter, ironically around the same time I began working at a regional bank branch. Leading up to the day he asked me to leave, there had been no indication. Every week for a year, in earnest, I filled out application after application until one day I decided to lie on one, because the truth wasn't getting me where I needed to go. That application was the one for the bank, and I invented a work history that correlated with the job description in perfect detail. The next day, they called for an interview, and within a week I started bank- teller training. This happened to coincide nicely with my eviction from Todd's house. In his opinion, I had been taking advantage of the situation far too long and was abusing his kindness by being lazy. Pride would not let me argue, because when someone puts you out, it tends to be final; there would be no long, drawn-out *please let me stay.* I simply packed my bags and left.

Joseph lived in the same complex as Todd, except he didn't

have a lease and therefore paid no monthly rent, meaning he also had no electricity. Since it was approaching spring again, he didn't need heat. The apartment stayed lit by candlelight, creating an eerie ambiance. For three months, Joseph lived illegally, and no one from management said a word. He had a son with Todd's sister Shayla, and after their breakup, he remained close with the family even though he seemed to be the proverbial fuckup—the one always living underneath life, the weight just enormous enough to make him never want to do anything with himself. Joseph had shown me the small-city glitter of Lansing from time to time, and I was grateful for that. He appeared to generally be a good guy whom bad luck followed relentlessly, and he seemed unsurprised when I knocked on his door, asking for a place to crash. Apparently everyone, including Shayla and Diane, had known that I was doomed to be kicked out of Todd's house the day I stepped across the threshold.

Two weeks on the job at the bank, and I noticed a diminutive tear in the operation of business. Destiny can reveal itself in the most interesting intersections of a person's life: that's what I thought after entering c-r-a-i-g d-a-v-i-s in the database on a whim after lunch one day. The bank's archaic system had no way of tracking an inquiry made by a teller into a bank account. I had talked to Craig in Miami a few days earlier and decided to see what information popped up in terms of accounts with that name. The Craig Davis who resided in Iowa possessed so much money that I deduced it would be doubtful he'd miss ten thousand dollars in the span of a year. Mr. Davis received a statement twice a year and had not made an inquiry into his account in over five years, which seemed to help my odds. When I learned all of this, all bets were off, and the desire to leave Lansing became greater and obtainable. I was tired of being embarrassed and ashamed of living with Joseph in an abandoned apartment and sleeping on a floor cushioned by blankets and sheets until I could get enough money to change my direction. The direction became clearer when I thought about this bank account and Dollar Bill in Memphis.

That last time I had seen Dollar, I could have said no. *No* had formed on my lips, but I had failed to utter the word. In that split second, I could have summoned the courage, but I had not; I'd grabbed the glass pipe from his hands and pulled the smoke. That October night, I spent all the money I had chasing an elusive five-minute high. I owed him a thousand for cocaine he had given me on credit, and the guilt of owing that much money had brought me to the brink of suicide. It's like you wake up, and immediately something stirs inside your chest. You can't breathe, so you pull the covers over your head in an attempt to escape the world, but you gotta deal with this shit somehow, someway. The next morning my only option had been to go to the liquor store and cash the cashier's check written out to Howard University. The owner of the liquor store should not have cashed the check, but he knew me well and believed me when I said my parents had made a mistake and really wanted me to have the money. Up until that point, through trial and error, I had managed to accrue 101 credits, keeping a 2.25 grade point average. I needed 135 credits to graduate. Since I had already screwed King Freak out of his money, I convinced myself the only way to get out of the hole I'd dug for myself would be to buy an ounce from Cat Daddy and get fronted one. This way I could make a profit and pay King and Dollar Bill back their money. I'd still have to compensate Cat for the fronted ounce, and I could put my tuition bill from Howard off until the end of the semester. However, I'd defeated my own plans with that one final knockout blow of smoking up the entire product that disastrous December night with two women in Maryland.

Hollywood could not have scripted a better set of circumstances for the con that was about to play out in Lansing. A few factors were working in my favor. One: in 1985, the bank had no formal computer system to track the accessed information back to me. Two: on Saturdays, I floated to other branches and worked with people who did not see each other during the week. Three: when a customer showed his or her identification, the only person who could see if I wrote down the correct license information would be me. Four: any transaction over three thousand dollars had to be okayed by the branch manager with a signature. These four points made it virtually impossible for the bank to determine fault. This was how I explained it to Dollar over the phone. I just needed a warm body for active participation in my scheme.

The branch manager never saw the play. She only saw a well-dressed African American male, perhaps in his early twenties, standing in a long-suffering line along with the rest of the customers—because on Saturdays there was always a line. She saw him go to teller three. After a brief period, she saw the teller leave his station and return presenting a withdrawal slip for ten thousand dollars. The slip was properly filled out with the customer's driver's license information. The branch manager will leave out the fact that she never saw the driver's license, because she never sees the driver's license. The surveillance tape will confirm the branch manager's testimony, and the bank will be—and still is—at a loss as to the identity of the Craig Davis who showed up that Saturday morning. I wish I could tell you that I had felt sympathetic toward the Craig Davis in Iowa who would eventually discover an unauthorized withdrawal, but I didn't. In my mind, I needed the money more than he did.

Perhaps the most anxious I have been in my life was the wait until one in the afternoon when I got off work. The mere fact that I had entrusted someone to hold ten thousand dollars of which the majority belonged to me kept me watching the clock minute by minute, then second by second. With sweat running down my face and my heart racing, I trotted across the parking lot to the blue rental car. Joseph and Dollar were in the front seat, grinning because the plan went smooth.

For giving me somewhere to stay when I needed it the most, I gave Joseph a thousand dollars. Joseph dropped off the rental car. Dollar Bill and I left Lansing's Greyhound Bus Station around midnight headed to Memphis first, then on to Florida to cop blow from my good ol' Craig Davis, who was back in Miami moving weight. No need for conversation between Dollar Bill and myself. The tires' indelible *hum* carried our mediation far into the night.

After returning to DC from Miami, Cat Daddy helped me secure a job as a mail clerk at a telecommunications company on 19th Street and L Streets. He worked in the accounts payable department, and we had started doing business again when Craig got arrested for selling a kilo of powder to undercover federal agents in a Prince George's County shopping plaza. All had been forgiven with Cat Daddy, and I handled my second stint in DC much better, as I quit freebasing and only snorted. I rented a townhouse in Alexandria and drove a candy apple red convertible Fiat Spyder.

Craig had been smuggling drugs through customs from Eleuthera and then driving up I-95 to deal in DC. Before his arrest, we rarely did business together because I didn't have clientele on his level. However, Cat Daddy and I worked well, and he kept me supplied enough to make a decent living. He had become a supplier through his father in New York. His father's connection in South America would fly cocaine up to JFK inside dead bodies. He had an operation behind the door of a bodega on Nostrand Avenue in Brooklyn. Also behind the door—if one was lucky enough to get that far—were slot machines, poker tables, and crap games. Cat Daddy would take me to New York with him sometimes on the weekends after work to their stash house on Herkimer. It was Cat's job to cut and package the cocaine. His pops mostly sold hundred-dollar packages and could sell a broken-down kilo in less than a week, sometimes two days. Cat would always leave with no less than two ounces for his work, which we would sell in DC.

Over the phone at work, Reginald, the man who called my father "pop" and me "brother," said, "quit that fuckin' job and meet me at Miami International." My father had become a mentor to Reginald in high school after Reginald had accidentally shot and killed a friend while playing with a loaded shotgun. I trusted Reginald when he yelled *quit* into the receiver, so it took all of thirty seconds to leave behind the daily task of sorting interoffice and postal mail into wooden slots. I walked into my supervisor's office and said, "I quit." In a way, I would miss the mail runs, where I often stopped in a select few administrative secretaries' offices, closed the door, and did a couple of lines with them. Cocaine had infiltrated its way into corporate America. These were people with houses, mortgages, and car notes. They held college degrees—advanced degrees—and they were upwardly mobile professionals. I had customers on every floor throughout the twenty-five-story building.

My flight from National landed on time and I took the escalator toward our agreed-upon meeting terminal on the lower level. Reginald's burgundy Kangol gliding over a partition toward the connecting gate caught my attention. I yelled his name until, finally, he turned around. I still could not believe he had married Arinique, Craig's cousin. Arinique Ferguson had grown up in Hatchet Bay, Eleuthera, the place Craig often referred to as a hotbed of activity for smugglers. She and Reginald met when I brought him to Miami with me to buy five pounds of weed. Since Craig's seven-year incarceration on drug trafficking charges, I had been trying to find a way to get down there and meet some of his connections, and Reginald's marriage to Arinique opened the door. Reginald had visited and talked with Arinique's father, who assured him he could get cocaine at a cheap price. He had done so for Craig's father many times. Between us, we had twenty-five hundred dollars and a hope and a prayer we could buy a half a kilo. This trip would be the gateway to a never-ending brooklet of cash.

While Reginald was reserved and apprehensive, I'd been waiting for this moment since I had first heard about this small island in the Bahamas. I understood the escalation to the next level in terms of the drug trade. I was getting ready to do something few dealers had ever done. Forget about standing on the corner or going to buy from someone else. I wanted to be that someone else.

The trip began in an Aero Coach propeller aircraft. Adrenaline raced through my ribcage as I walked along the tarmac. It was difficult to contain the intense excitement. I asked the pilot, and he agreed to let me sit in the copilot's seat. This presented the illusion that I somehow had charge of the aircraft in case we made a sudden landing in the ocean or to an uncharted island. The circular instrumentation, the gears and levers in the cockpit, fascinated me, and I was enthusiastic to observe how the pilot navigated the plane.

Upon takeoff, the air turned noticeably thick, and the sun washed the sky indigo. We elevated through a fading horizon. When the plane ascended into the clouds at a phenomenal rate of speed, I felt those same surges of adrenaline distribute throughout my body. This was the first time I had ever been high without a mood-altering substance. I peered curiously down from an altitude of twenty thousand feet, enchanted by the sturdiness of the dark blue Atlantic, which in time gave way to the crystal glass of the Caribbean. Until I did some research, I'd never known that the Bahamas was saturated with over nine hundred islands. However, it was the little-known Eleuthera that held my interest. The island stretches two hundred fifty miles north to south, but is only two miles at its widest point.

We approached Eleuthera from the north. From inside the plane, the only concrete images I could identify were canopies of palm trees straddling one strip of road, with tiny villagers walking alongside the edges. The pilot tilted the wings starboard and we circled the township of Lower Bogue twice, like an errant gull, before gliding smoothly onto a tiny airstrip. Exiting the aircraft, the tropical warmth of the island wrapped its tentacles around our bodies and, at that moment, I knew I was on foreign soil, hundreds of miles away from anything USA. In a way, I was half-expecting girls in grass skirts and maybe a drink with a little umbrella in it. But that didn't happen.

After showing our birth certificates and identification to clear customs, Reginald and I secured a car rental from one of the local taxi drivers and headed south to the township of Hatchet Bay. The streets veering off the main road through the island were poorly paved, and I actually witnessed people walking barefoot. Coming from the states, I could not fully comprehend the concept of not wearing shoes. How does one negotiate the ragged rocks and broken glass? I pushed my face out the open window and allowed the wind to jet stream against my face. I inhaled the low brush and high palm trees. The calmness of the wind mellowed my senses, and I was at rare peace. Since Reginald had been here before, he drove, skillfully maneuvering the tight corners while hugging the left side of the asphalt road.

Suddenly, he made a right off the main road, which had seemed to go on forever, into a small township with houses painted various pastel shades—blue, yellow, rose. There was a harbor to the right docked with different size fishing boats. Reginald steered the car into a smaller road lined with palmettos until we came to rest in front of a small house level with the sea. In front of the house, there were three palm trees, their trunks rising from the sand like the three tines of a pitchfork.

"Welcome to 'leuthra, mon," the caramel-skinned Bahamian of about fifty-five said while motioning his lanky arms for us to exit our rental and join him on the patio. Daniel, Arinique's father, had a half-pint of Grand Marnier on the patio table. We got out of the car and shook his hand. He smelled like maybe he had been a fisherman all his life. The waves from the sea were coming in, steady, methodical, tranquil.

"Goddamn, Reggie. What take you so damn long to get back here? Eh? I been waitin and waitin here, tryin to get tings together for you and you takin your sweet Jesus time." Daniel stared back out at the sea. This was his meditation.

Reginald countered with, "Daniel, now you know I had to get that money together. Can't buy nothing without no money. Now, I got somebody here with me. This here Craig's friend from DC. Him and Craig went to school together. Matter of fact, I met your daughter through him." Daniel waved for me to sit down next to him. I took a seat and relished the expansive, crystal blue Caribbean that Daniel was privileged with seeing every morning.

"Well goddamn why ain't you say so, boy? If you friend to Craig den you friend to Daniel."

We sat on the front porch discussing how we were going to cop and whom we would cop from. Although Daniel claimed we had missed several opportunities, we still should be able to get a good deal somewhere on the island. I kept thinking the sooner we got back with product, the sooner we could return. I would come to learn there is no such thing as *soon* in Eleuthera. Waiting was a way of life.

Daniel proceeded to give us a tour of this coastal town, where the soft white sand reaches out to touch the effervescent blue sea as if they were longtime lovers, as if commingling was manifest destiny. Our first intermediary stop was Club Let Me Remember, located on the main road of Hatchet Bay. Over drinks, Daniel explained to us that most people he knew only sold kilos, and we probably would have to search a while to find someone who would break a kilo in half. After two drinks with some of the local citizens, we left the club and journeyed to James Cistern, a fishing village begging for any kind of economic development. What I found unique about James Cistern was that all the houses in the township faced the sea. The town's main square was small and, from its center, you could observe homemade stands by the sea where people sold conch salad or grouper. There were several tables under palm trees where the elderly played checkers. When we exited the vehicle, mosquitoes bombarded us in every direction, kamikaze style. Reginald and I swatted furiously while Daniel remained oblivious to the onslaught. We swatted while walking to the village bar to order more drinks. Daniel ordered Grand Marnier.

Everybody knew Daniel, but nobody had cocaine. Frustrated, we left JC and made the forty-minute ride to Governor's Harbour, the capital of Eleuthera. Hugging shoreline and from the left side of the road, the water stayed forever blue. The only traffic light on the island swung on a cable wire in the center of Governor's, a tourist township where the rich landed million-dollar airplanes on private airstrips. You could get supplies, boat rentals, do banking and a host of other activities that were not possible in other townships. Sailboats and small yachts lay moored with multicolored sails, projecting rainbow shadows in the water. We stopped at the local bar for more drinks. Daniel appeared more interested in showing off his American friends than copping drugs.

"No problem, mon. We gettin de stuff soon. Soon comin boy yeah I tell you." I wanted to cuss his *soon comin boy yeah I tell you* ass out, but I reserved my anger and hoped for the best.

With no legal speed limit between townships, we covered ground quickly. Tarpum Bay, with its turquoise houses on the hillside, goats bleating and running aimlessly through town, is by far the most scenic township on the island. By nightfall, we were easing toward Rock Sound, and Daniel was easing further into drunkenness. Along the road, there were people with flashlights hunting sand crab. The crab is drawn to the light, captured, and then sold to local restaurants and bars. With Reginald just as liquored up as Daniel, I long ago had assumed driver duties, as I no longer trusted Daniel behind the wheel. While we sailed down the unlit road at sixty, Daniel motioned for me to pull over toward a building with a billboard that read: WELCOME TO BIG MARY'S.

Full-figured Big Mary welcomed the Americans (as everybody on the island had begun to call us) with open arms. We ordered cracked conch, peas and rice, and Beck's. Big Mary was having a special on shellfish, plus music was playing, so the place was packed. Mary's reminded me of my grandmother's jook joint in Birmingham, where people would come to eat, drink, and have a good time. On impulse, I offered to help bartend. "Friend of Daniel a friend of mine," Mary sighed with relief, walking back through the swinging doors to the kitchen. I glanced across the room to Daniel, who by this time was in a serious stupor, slurring his speech, giving everybody within earshot his history as a fisherman and taxi driver. I was overhearing his instructions on how to throw sticks of dynamite in the sea to knock jackfish unconscious when Reginald motioned for me to come to the booth where he was eating. He introduced me to a freckle-faced guy sitting across from him. I looked down in Reginald's hands and there was a brown bag, which he handed to me partially open, and I inhaled nothing but sweet-smelling bud. Reginald had bought a quarter-pound of weed for twenty-five dollars. We stepped out into the parking lot, where the opaque sky deepened the glow of a moon whose aura penetrated the palm leaves and projected pinstripe shadows on our faces. We rolled a spliff and smoked until we coughed. By the time we finished, I was paranoid. Crickets ground banjo songs, and some unidentifiable bird punctuated the swirls of the sea. Constellations of stars appeared to be dancing, and I knew I was high as hell.

Riding through the black splat of night from which we came, the moon remained suspended in its crescent pose, idle. On the island after dark, the sky is expansive—as if one is at the beginning of the world—even in its opaqueness. If it were not for the drone of tires, it would be difficult to debate whether we were moving down a two-lane road—the *hum* and reality. The depression I felt wasn't about drugs or the *hum*. It was more about me missing Chrissy in the states—Chrissy lying on my king size bed in my condo, all alone, waiting.

Chrissy and I had remained friends since our Howard days. She was the kind of girl who fit the bourgeoisie role but also railed against it. As in, Chrissy could be the one at the wine-and-cheese gathering, complete with black Coach riding boots, having just pulled up in a drop-top, candy apple Volkswagen Cabriolet before holding court about the poisons of class and how wealth don't mean nothing if you aren't using it to help people. That was Chrissy— always critiquing a capitalistic system that created division. When I had returned back to DC, we had started dating, and being with Chrissy made me feel like I had something in life to look forward to. She worked at an architectural design firm, was responsible and fine. However, my drug life had begun to take a toll on our relationship because I was always away conducting deals; I stood her up when we made dates, and she worried about me selling drugs internationally. Chrissy kept telling me over and over: *this can't last forever.* I could tell she was tiring of a never-there boyfriend.

This can't last forever kept flashing in the backdrop of a black sky as I began to reflect on one of my early childhood lessons regarding women. In 1973, my best friend and neighbor Peter's oldest brother Snake, after drinking a bottle of Thunderbird, demonstrated to us the correct way to slow drag with a girl. Snake managed this maneuver with the imaginary silhouette of a woman in the middle of the basement floor. He rested each hand on imaginary hipbones while Marvin Gaye talked bout how he been *trying to hold back this feeling for so long.* Peter and I watched carefully—our twelve-year-old pupils absorbing every movement. Snake philosophized in careful dialogue that the premise to slow dragging with a woman was simply to dip the hips twice to each side, allowing the hands to guide the movement. You always want to lean—this was crucial. He said, *you gotta pull the woman to you, let her know who in charge, but at the same time, young bloods, you gotta be gentle wit dat thang.*

For fifteen years I practiced and perfected the art of *being gentle wit dat thang* as taught by Snake, and one night after a party at my house in Alexandria, months after I'd gotten back to DC from Lansing, I put on Marvin for Chrissy so he could ask *if you feel like I feel.* Chrissy and I gravitated to the middle of the basement floor, swayed by lead guitar but more by childhood memory and, *come on, come on.* We intersected as if instinctual. Marvin begged, and I pulled Chrissy tight. She allowed me to lead, and I gripped, dipped her torso like Snake instructed those many years ago. Something kinetic—an electrical exchange between bodies. We pulled even closer and kissed long after the record stopped—the needle begging to be lifted from the vinyl. *This can't last forever.*

That night, I drove back to Hatchet Bay high and angry that we didn't make a connection. I silently wondered if Daniel would be able to hold up his end of the bargain. We had been to six townships and not one whiff of cocaine—only a bunch of talk. Here I was in a foreign country, tripping off the dark oceanic sky, watching black crabs lug their cumbersome bodies alongside the road, hypnotized by the blinding lights from oncoming cars. Doubt set in. I was here on a busted wing, a prayer, and a shoestring budget.

The melody of the sea washing up against uneven coral reef—I awoke to this. Each incoming wave a separate meditation within itself, the phosphorous foam accenting the echo. Disenchanted by the day before, I got out of bed before anyone else and drove to Gregory Town alone to eat breakfast at a small hotel. The restaurant was empty, and I was able to get a table next to a window soaking up the morning. I ordered fish head and grits with a bottle of beer. After I finished eating, I wanted to investigate something I had observed from the previous day. Coming from the airport, we had passed right through Gregory Town, and I'd noticed a group of young Bahamian men with dreads smoking weed in front of a small oval-shaped, one-room house. I paid for my food and walked up the paved road. Two men were sitting on a giant sea turtle shell. I walked through the open gate and introduced myself. The two guys nodded their heads but said nothing. I then told them I was visiting as a guest of Daniel's from Hatchet Bay and was new to the island. The mentioning of Daniel's name relaxed their posture.

"Why didn you say mon? We know you ain from here. You gotta be 'merican. Dis here be my brudda Stefrey and everybody here call me Franz. Welcome to the island, boss." Franz appeared to be the older of the two. He stuck out his hand.

Sometimes one gets a sense about the order of things in a new environment. My intuition told me that these two men knew about the white powder I wanted to purchase. The large cigarette boats parked on both sides of their small house sort of helped put things in perspective. By the time we shared a couple of beers and smoked a couple of joints, we were laughing like old friends, which gave me the courage to mention I wanted to spend two grand for a half-kilo of powder. Franz and Stefrey laughed in my face, the kind of laughter that had one doubled-over, holding one's stomach, wiping tears away and gasping for breath, and then laughing again—an infectious laughter willing the unsuspected victim (me) to join the fray, while the reason is not totally clear.

"Boy lemme tell you someting. Two grand aint nothin, see. Whole keys, don' be breakin nothin down, you know? Too much trouble for sure. We sail over to South America two, tree times a month with more coke than you can dream. Two grand? Boy lemme tell you something, cause see, I like you, mon. See like you is cool, plus Daniel and me is alright, so check this."

On the outskirts of Hatchet Bay, there is an abandoned chicken and cow slaughterhouse off the one main road shielded by acreages of green foliage. Five hours after talking to the brothers, Reginald, Daniel, and I were in a car with the engine idling softly, waiting.

"I was gonna see dem today you know," Daniel told me, and I thought to myself, *Why not yesterday, Daniel?*

When the brothers came swerving around the corner of the dirt road in their drop-top red Corvette, pulled up next to our car, and tossed a whole kilo to me in the passenger's seat, I was speechless. I knew a kilo cost five grand; I only had two. Sensing my stress level go up, Franz told me to give him the two thousand and bring the balance the next time I came—in other words, he was fronting me the other half. He trusted me to come back. They left in screeching tires and loud music, knowing full well there were no police on the island to stop them.

I could not gaze into the tea leaves nor read the tarot cards, so I did not know my fortune, nor would I be able to stop the loop-de-loop I was about to ride on. Friends would betray friends; families would be broken, disconnected, almost beyond repair. Lovers would be lost to the white lady's pull of money and power and other lovers who only cared about using you up—this was what cocaine did. The United States would become a playground: Memphis, Birmingham, Atlanta, DC, and New York, after which, hopping on and off of planes, riding in new cars, and attending black-tie events would become memories, and sleeping in cars, standing in soup lines, and stealing just to eat a meal would replace them as my life. Lacking the insight and fortitude to play the tape forward, I rewound the tape and reflected on all the times I had had to struggle for money. In the back room of Daniel's house, Reginald and I broke down the kilo in halves and then smaller portions to strap to our bodies to avoid detection.

The cocaine epidemic had been in full effect for five years when we boarded the airplane back to Miami International. Women were prostituting themselves for a small pebble to smoke in a glass. Black men further estranged themselves from their families. Cocaine wreaked havoc in America. It would be two decades before the total devastation wrought by crack cocaine became clear. I did not have the vision to understand this when I walked through United States Customs and gave the agent my declaration card. I was about to further contribute to the self-destruction of a people I claimed to love. The customs agent barely glanced at my baggy shorts draped by a double-XL T-shirt. She refused to see what was strapped to my body because she couldn't really see me. She chose to keep me invisible among the hundreds of people who passed through her line daily to gain entrance to the United States. Same for Reginald, and I knew I would never strap cocaine to my body again, because I didn't want to be the one sweating bullets in a US Customs line. From this point on, I would pay other people. Soon, there would be baggage handlers to load the suitcases and take them off, both in Eleuthera and Miami. Then too, there would be boats coming to the states, planes flying low, and I would be sucked into a world that would refuse to release me from its clutches.

Fishing boat! Green Castle, Cyril blurted in spasmodic breaths running down the dirt road from Batelco, a fancy name for phone house. He told me to get up from the patio chair and, *get in. DEA fucked up.* We sped south from Tarpum Bay in a four-door '78 LTD, damn near hyperventilating. Cyril had just gotten off the phone with a friend, almost certain the ship moored in Green Castle was loaded with kilos. The DEA had not found the secret compartment after a routine search and had left the boat moored on the docks to be impounded. We needed to get to Green Castle like *right then* and somehow get aboard. Cyril estimated close to one hundred kilos in a hidden compartment.

I came to know Cyril on my third trip to the island, when we became friends through Franz and Stefrey. My relationship with Reginald had deteriorated, so I struck out solo and began coming to the island by myself. Franz and Stefrey were going on hiatus, preparing for their yearly fishing expedition, and they invited me to come along with them; however, I could not fathom living on a boat for six months, pulling up fish from the bottom of an ocean. I wasn't schooled in nautical navigation, and that was a whole lotta water to drink. But the brothers introduced me to Cyril, an Eleutheran transplant from Cat Island.

Cyril had possessed a small shipment of wet cocaine ditched by a cigarette boat being chased by the coast guard and picked up by a friend taking a morning walk near Savannah Sound. Cyril showed me how to cut the coke with mannitol so it would dry and at the same time retain most of its potency. He charged me fifteen hundred dollars, which was a bargain price for a kilo. This was a couple years before the crack epidemic appeared on the streets of urban cities and then seeped into the hillsides of rural America. I thought about selling it already cooked up in freebase form, which would have been easier since it was wet, but reasoned that not too many people would buy it that way; I had customers who liked to snort.

After that initial encounter, Cyril came to the states to visit. He never told me, but based on Stefrey and Franz's methodology, I would say that Cyril stashed five kilos into a dummy motor and ran one motor from Eleuthera to the port of Miami. When US Customs came aboard the ship, they probably ignored the two engines. In any event, Cyril drove to DC from Miami, and I was able to wholesale kilos at eighteen thousand. Acting as the middleman, I made two thousand per transaction. Cyril brought his wife and spent a week exploring Adams Morgan, DuPont Circle, Columbia Heights, and Georgetown. They rode the yellow line from King Street and stood outside the White House with their I LOVE DC T-shirts. No one would suspect that they had just smuggled cocaine into the United States.

It was a year later that I found myself in that LTD, more excited than even Cyril. Pulling into Green Castle, the road split in two directions—one headed west along the Cape Eleuthera peninsula in the Caribbean, the other due south toward Eleuthera Point and the turbulent collision of the Atlantic and the Caribbean. We followed the peninsula until we reached the docks, only to find a feeding frenzy on one fishing vessel. Moonlight glittered off the sea, illuminating a well-organized operation of extraction.

Swimming portside, a Bahamian named Andres snuck aboard the ship and propelled himself onto the vessel. He had received the same information as Cyril—only sooner. Andres crept below deck and searched until he located the trap door and the biggest illegal payday in Green Castle history. He found not one, but two hundred kilos of cocaine. This is what the boy of no more that twelve told us, trotting away from the scene with a single kilo wrapped in fiberglass tucked in the crook of his arm. Cyril and I parked and watched our dream wither away with the tide, as we were perhaps an hour too late. The only comfort came when we talked to Andres after observing the recovery. Since Cyril and Andres knew each other from way back, Cyril's head nod was enough to secure four kilos as long as I paid for one up front, which came to five thousand. I don't know if you would call that a silver lining, but the trip back north was not a total wash.

When Reginald and Arinique held their formal wedding in Hatchet Bay a year after their courthouse marrige, he and I rented a plane to Nassau; then we rented a yacht and sailed around the island like we were its proprietors. I brought Chrissy along, and the four of us rode scooters by the hour, exploring the narrow streets lined with multihued houses. Chrissy wasn't impressed with money; she only wanted me to stop because *this can't last forever*. That night, riding back to Tarpum Bay, I craved Marvin in my head instead of *can't last forever*, knowing our relationship had disintegrated.

The following Christmas and New Year's holiday, Daniel came to DC to visit. This would be the first time he saw how I operated. At that point, I mostly sold wholesale, and not much in the DMV area; most of my money came from visits to Birmingham and Memphis with Dollar Bill. The people closest to me were the people from Alabama, my homeboys. Cat Daddy and I shared a house on Buchanan Street in Alexandria where we kept drugs and money, but we lived elsewhere. The house was unassuming red brick in a row of unassuming red brick houses. We had a few guys from Alabama who operated locally, but nothing too serious. The house was a place we went to watch football games, cook out, and have parties. The main premise of our existence was to make sure everyone could pay rent and live well. I never stepped outside this circle of friends. This was the uncomplicated network Daniel arrived to in December.

Money flowed through the money machines, and life was good, but my father once told me that *everybody ain't happy for you.* Almost always, there is a rat stirring in the woodwork, a pair of eyes plotting. After being the proverbial fuckup, I now determined who got paid and who didn't, who ate and who didn't. I was the one they had to come to to ask, and not everybody was happy with that. Daniel became the wild card, the unsuspecting joker in a spades game. Someone slid up to Daniel while he drank cognac and pushed blow up his nose, and whispered: *Say, jack, what is it really like down that joint? Hook can't be treating you right. He giving you money? You know we got money? Say, jack, we got these girls you should meet.* But I knew none of this because I was running around thinking we one big happy family. Daniel think we one big happy family too and yielded to their requests. I flew to Birmingham and left Daniel in the hands of my trusted friends—the ones I swore by, and they stuck the pointed tip of their jealousy in my back as soon as I left.

With that said, I was not the man walking through customs strapped. As a matter of fact, no one I knew was supposed to be walking through customs. But someone was. In the week I was gone from DC, Mac, my homeboy from Montgomery—though more a lieutenant for Cat Daddy, with whom he plotted to go behind my back—went to Eleuthera without me. Mac could not feel the eyes watching him as he exited the twin-engine plane, didn't know the eyes never stopped watching as he first took a shuttle, then a monorail. When he fell asleep on the monorail, and the strapped package became unloosened and slipped through his short pants, he would realize his last mistake. I have never asked him, but I wonder: did he understand, as the customs officials escorted him to the back room where he would begin the process that led to a ten-year prison sentence, that I rejoiced in his deliberate betrayal of going to Eleuthera behind my back?

Two years after the double cross had forced me to stay away, I returned to Eleuthera with my homeboy from Birmingham, Stump Walker. Mac's arrest was the first in a series of events that altered the drug landscape in Eleuthera. Cyril took a chance against my advice and wound up getting arrested in Alabama for conspiracy to distribute. Franz was indicted by the Bahamian government and given five years. Stefrey refused to operate without Franz, returned to fishing full time, and built a mansion just outside Hatchet Bay. Andres got locked up on a sting operation. Daniel barely wanted to talk.

Stump wanted to take a chance despite this recent history, and I needed income, which had been drying up, especially since I split with Cat Daddy when I found out he had gone to Eleuthera behind my back. Since we had history, and he had forgiven me long ago for running off with his package, I found myself able to look past it, but I knew our friendship had taken a serious hit. Cat eventually went back to dealing with his pops in New York while I waited for the heat to cool down on the island.

Upon arrival in Eleuthera, Stump and I settled at an inn, and I contacted Daniel, who felt betrayed by Mac and Cat Daddy. The island had taken on a different identity, and I no longer felt comfortable and confident. I was made to wait until people could be sure I was not the police looking to set them up.

Stump did not handle the wait well. He tired of going to Club Let Me Remember for jackfish and peas and rice, or to Kristiano's in Gregory Town for grouper and grits. He soon lost interest in the tongue souse and cracked conch from Big Mary's and demanded to fly to Nassau and deal with some people he knew. He did not want to walk the white-sanded beaches, nor was he interested in snorkeling in the Atlantic. *Soon-coming* became a dirty word. Stump could not understand why he should wait so long. I left with him for Nassau, knowing all he needed to do was sit tight a few more days, cause don't nobody rush for nothing on Eleuthera. However, before we left, Stefrey did give me the number of his youngest brother who lived in Nassau.

We caught Bahamas Air and landed early on a Monday in an attempt to blend with other tourists entering the island. Since we were already in the Bahamas, there was no need to clear customs. We were stunned when a Bahamian official walked up, asked us to step into the bathroom, and body searched us for drugs, which he did not find. However, the official did question Stump about the wad of money he had strapped to his waist, which was less than ten thousand, and legal. The search shook us a bit because we did not expect it. Leaving the airport, I suggested to Stump we go see Stefrey's brother. I wanted to talk to someone who knew the island.

Stefrey's brother, Drake, would sell us a kilo for a thousand dollars more than we would have paid on Eleuthera, but he would also sail us back to Eleuthera in his fishing boat. He had to go that way to get to Cat Island and knew that there was intense security at Nassau airport. If at all possible, no one smuggled through Nassau, the main reason being you had to clear customs before taking off, so you were dealing with two agencies—coupled with the fact that Nassau was a tourist attraction. Stump declined his offer, stating that he wanted to check out his own connection.

We left Drake's boat repair shop with Drake driving to the address Stump provided. While we waited in the van, I asked Drake about the goings-on in Eleuthera. We talked about what Mac's arrest meant to the island, how the DEA and coast guard were making concerted efforts to disrupt the actions of anyone involved in drugs. Even though Franz had gone to prison, they'd managed to save money.

Before I could mention that Stump was taking too long, he hopped back in the van and told us everything was cool. He'd only bought one kilo, and it was strapped to the middle part of his body at that very moment. I wanted to inform him of his idiocy. We were taking chances we didn't have to take.

Drake made a right, and then we rounded the left curve and came to the airport parking lot. Once the van engine turned off, Stump slid the side door open and he and I hopped out the front. Within a split second of us thanking Drake, a car rounding the left curve accelerated, then stopped and parked behind us. Six men got out of a late model Ford and surrounded Stump.

I could tell by the bewilderment on Stump's face that these were the same men who had sold him the package strapped to his body. When Drake closed his door, I glanced over, but before I could turn back around, Stump bolted through the loose semi-circle with head down, body low and square. Damn boy ran for everything his momma a gave him—life. He cleared all arm's reach, but those same arms rearranged themselves in swift pursuit without hesitation. Stump ran in wide, arcing circles, trying to avoid capture, each time expanding his circumference, occasionally darting a straight line and then zigzagging in desperation. How could one utter the word help? Couldn't call the average citizen—and damn sure couldn't call the police. Quandary might be the right word. Stuck in a moving picture. Suspended.

One guy stayed by the van and held his elbow chest-high to me as if to prevent the contemplation of retaliation. Drake did not move. Not a breathing human in sight. Odds dictated I freeze and watch those chasing arms grab Stump about the waist, stopping and then twirling his torso. He could've been in a modern ballet, ripped shirt and all. But more importantly, the package tore, and white powder trailed Stump everywhere he was flung. Call it Theatre of the Absurd. Call it early American vaudeville. To call it a rag doll disintegrating into yarn does not do the metaphor justice. It took one minute for the five men to take the package off Stump's body, leaving him swinging, clutching, and grabbing at the wind. Stump resurrected himself from the ground, dazed and breathless. No police. We hopped back in the van, negotiating the curve at almost fifty, not in pursuit, but in *gettin ghost*. We were victim and perpetrator at the same time.

Two days later in Miami on 135th and 22nd Avenue, also known as Opa Locka or "The Locks," I relayed the story of how Stump spun around, scattering a kilo of cocaine across the parking lot's asphalt, to Craig in his living room. Craig had been out of federal prison one week, and this was the conversation I least expected to have with him. I retold the sequence of events of how Cat Daddy had betrayed me, and how Stump hadn't wanted to wait so he ended up going to Nassau and getting robbed. "Unbelievable," Craig kept telling me after I repeated each detail of the robbery at least twice. "Unbelievable. And you waiting on dude to come back from Birmingham with more money. Are you serious?"

I knew it sounded crazy that Stump was still trying to score. Once we had arrived in Miami, Stump went back to Alabama to retrieve more money to recoup the loss. If he was careful and got a good deal in Miami, then he could squeeze a profit, plus throw something my way. This is what happens when one becomes desperate. I longed for those adrenaline moments again, so I ignored my better judgment and agreed to wait in Miami. I had become as desperate as he.

The tropical climate made it easier to embrace the Magic City as a second home. I was enamored with its welcoming warmth, the bright pastel architecture, the red-clay ceramic tiles and the flatness of the landscape, which stretches to the edge of the ocean. I loved the palm and orange trees and the canals that snaked their way behind people's homes.

Poverty and wealth were distributed unequally. This became evident when riding down Ali Baba and 22nd Avenue, where the rolodex of black and brown images blended with the run-down houses and storefronts hugging the cracked sidewalks. There was a laughter and sadness, a compilation of joy and sorrow in the sounds that escorted one throughout neighborhoods like Opa Locka and Liberty City, which were just coming out of the race riots of the mid-eighties. There was a sense that you were at the edge, or the beginning, of the world.

Two days after I told Craig about the incident at the airport in Nassau, I sat in a run-down projects apartment a stone's throw from the Orange Bowl. The lights were not turned on, and the orange-reddish sun was bleeding faint light through venetian blinds that were covered in the soft film of cooking grease from the stove. I thought about five hundred dollars, the crack that further stretched the divide between Stump and me. Five hundred dollars turned out to be the magic number when Stump had come back with ten grand and refused to deal with Craig. For ten thousand five hundred dollars, Craig would have gone to his father and gotten us a little more than a half a kilo. His father still had his connections with the Cubans, and being that Craig had only been out of jail for a few days, he needed the money.

Instead, I was in the living room on a brown, worn couch that sagged in the middle, surveying the apartment while we waited on the person called to bring half a kilo for ten thousand dollars. In the kitchen sink, dishes were piled in a ceramic and plastic mountain. A tricycle with only one wheel on the back leaned against what was supposed to be a dining room table, only it was a card table with an ashtray and a pack of opened cigarettes on top. In this business, I had learned that one must always think something is stirring in the woodpile. There is always a rat, a cockroach, or some other indestructible rodent or pest in the background. It was the only thing I had been certain of in thirty-three years of living on earth. From the time I had learned to walk, there was always some figure that told me to keep my guard up, to anticipate. Pugilist might be a better word. Stick and move. Jab. Sidestep. Rope-a-dope. React. Combinate.

I got up, walked to the window, and our car was still parked in its spot. The parking lot was abandoned. I went back to the couch and sat down. *Something in the milk ain't clean. Can't be.* Stump watching television like he right at the crib. I wanted to ask if he needed a damn pillow and a drink, but instead I prepared to tell him I was out. Gone. Ghost. As in I *hadda feeling.* Soon as I *hadda that feeling,* the front door burst open, and seven men entered with automatic weapons and handguns meant to blow a muthafucka two universes past kingdom come. This is how life stops and turns on a dime in a split second. One second before, we had been breathing a little bit easier, thinking of some future event. And just like that, we were now contemplating how we were going to die.

There is always one in the pack itching to pull the curve of a trigger. Maybe he had no father; maybe his mother sold her body for crack; maybe his need for money superseded our need; maybe he was having a bad day, and the assurance that someone could pay for his struggle was the impetus for him to bullet-hole us into oblivion. *Please don't squeeze the trigger,* I wanted to say, but I could not. It would've been cowardice because, in my world, men had to take whatever life gave them. Tears and begging spoke of the weak. No room for emotion and compassion and tenderness and fear. Had to *take it like a man* before I graduated from crawling to walking. AKs, MAC-10s, nine millimeters, and .44 longs were locked and loaded on our skulls. I reclined on the sofa, knowing this would be my last day on earth.

Bitch set us up. Fucked around, and we in the trick bag. *Slipped* was what we did. Caught with our pants down below the kneecaps. Instead of the police, we got the stick-up boys. Death rattling hard at the door, and we had to figure something out— right here, right now, or tomorrow would be whatever memory we left behind. One of the men walked over and placed the open end of his .357 to my temple, and I was suddenly transported back to my grandmother's green clapboard house. Men and women playing spades, drinking red liquor in Dixie Cups, and listening to the jukebox recapitulate a certain kind of blues one can only know growing up in Alabama. Smoke so thick you can cut it with a butter knife. I am ten, and Bo Willie, my grandmother's boyfriend, is yelling at her because she is yelling at him for drinking too much liquor. He raised his fist like he wanted to hit her, and I remember I wanted to shoot him with a gun. However, all I had was a homemade rubber-band shooter. I imagined tying a clothespin to the tip of a fallen pecan branch, straining the rubber band until it latched in a cocked position. Then I imagined the rubber-band shooter as a sawed-off shotgun and when I squeezed the trigger, Bo Willie's chest exploded into a collage of red. One squeeze of the trigger and grandmother would be free. I had quickly dismissed the idea: I would never be capable of taking a human life. Guns killed, and I could not kill.

Unfortunately, the guy pointing the nickel-plated .357 at my head did not harbor the same feeling. He understood bang was forever, and if forever was where I needed to go for him to get that money, he would most happily help me get there. Clearly they wanted—no, needed—the ten thousand dollars wrapped around Stump's waist in a money sack. I wanted—no, needed—for this not to be the place where my dead body would be rolled onto a stretcher and into an ambulance. My mother could not get a call at eleven thirty on a Tuesday night with information that her only son was deader than a doorknob in a projects apartment in Northwest Miami.

Before the man spoke, I did—in a calm and measured manner. I told him we were unarmed and that, *it's yours baby boy.*

"Stump, give 'em the money," I calmly said, yet he looked at me and did not flinch. I repeated, "Stump, give them the money," and I could tell he was wrestling with the idea of being robbed—again. This trip had been nothing but disastrous from the get-go. How does one get robbed twice on a drug trip? The idea was to make money, not lose money. However, this was not the time to be a hero; all the heroes I knew were in the boneyard. His hesitation became too much, and I wanted to leap across the room and smack him for playing with my life. The man with the .357 pointed the barrel at Stump and asked, "Where dat money at?" This in turn excited the other men who had circled us; any gunfire would result in splattered skull and bone fragments sprayed everywhere. Someone among them wanted to kill us, I was certain.

The light bulb popped on in Stump's head. He rose up and slowly unbuttoned his shirt and slid the moneybag from around his waist. The guy holding the .357 walked over and grabbed it. He was looking at me now. *If you gonna shoot then shoot. Let's get this over with, right now. No, I will not beg for my life if that's what you want. These streets got me like they got you. Game recognize game. Shoot.* He could not hear my thoughts, but he knew. I still understood that one of these men pointing a gun craved pulling the trigger—there is always one. But that evening, the alpha male—the one who stops all movement when he speaks, the guy holding the .357, who has no problem boring a tunnel in a person's forehead—decided fair exchange, no robbery. No harm, no foul. Everything even-Steven. Tonight, we live.

5

SPACE AND TIME

DEAR LXXXX,

Because I promised. A change in locale allows us to understand there comes a moment before the defiance of gravity, when the pilot pulls back the control levers, commanding the twin engines toward a horizontal plane of fifteen thousand feet: that is freedom without uttering a word. Fifteen years I've been away from Eleuthera but never stopped speaking the island's name. As we depart the edge of the United States, the Atlantic spills past the future we conceive. For an hour and thirty minutes, there is a continuous drone of propellers circling clockwise, propelling us.

North Eleuthera is a private island shaped like a scythe, white sand lining the uneven coast. When nothing changes, nothing changes. Landing onto the small tarmac: the same green foliage, a line of Cessnas, single and twin, the customs house that reads WELCOME TO ELEUTHERA—all the same. Mateo is a grown man now, the DNA image of his father, Daniel, who died four years ago in an automobile accident on the main road that stretches two hundred fifty miles north to south. I was Mateo's age when I became friends with Daniel. Before heading to Hatchet Bay, we grab two Kaliks at the bar across from the terminal. Boy got Daniel R. Ferguson in him all the way. Drink first and talk later.

On the road, I remember the sudden turns, the houses. The makeshift vegetable and fruit stand between two coconut trees in Upper Bogue means take a left to Gregory Town. To the left, the dark blue, rugged Atlantic; the seductive Caribbean to the right, crystal clear, and the current sedates you. If there is a heaven, a state of being where everything copacetic—Kool and the Gang— well, this is it, and for a moment, I can't inhale. Nothing changes. This I remember. The right from Gregory Town to Hatchet Bay is always the same. The pastel houses, the cottage bars: Club Let Me Remember and Coral Reef. We take the left at Remember into a dog right curve, and then the panoramic view of the Caribbean Mateo grew up with. The sun, between thin gray clouds, is ready to morph day into calm night. Hattie, Daniel's widow, hugs me like a mother, and then hands me the keys to the small blue villa next to her house facing the sea. An hour later, Mateo and I walk the coral reef along the shoreline to Coral Reef, much like his father and I had. The son has assumed the father's footsteps; Dear Lxxxx, please follow mine.

We wake to the sun rising, the before-noon tide rushing in, soft and unhurried. Clouds splatter sporadically across the sky, and for a moment you hold your breath here and contemplate space and time. Immanuel Kant offers, *space is not a conception which has been derived from outward experiences*, so we can think of space as a set entity through which we experience life. What concerns me more is the idea of the object within space, and how this object is perceived with respect to aesthetic beauty. For Kant, the object is connected to sensibility, phenomena, and form. Only when the object is free of said conditions can it approach space (freedom). My alternative take is, what if we live with the maxim: *the object is inseparable from the condition.*

One could posit that, sitting between two coconut trees on a wooden bench, complete with table, the cerulean sea rolling straight at you is fixed. If space is a defined entity through which we operate, and if time is a byproduct of space, the two must coexist in a dichotomy where space supersedes time. We can be in space without time, but not time without space. Sitting here, between two coconut trees, how can I break free of this imagistic constraint, Lxxxx?

One of the ways would be to expand the lens through which I not only see myself sitting here, but note a man walking on the coral along the shore, kicking rotted coconuts. Oscillating the lens 180 degrees reveals small houses with wooden shutters propped, allowing the morning breeze to infiltrate the meshed window screens. Stray dogs wander throughout the settlement. None are aggressive, and two pups frolic along the beach, jumping in and out of the watery foam. Men prepare to crisscross the bay, fishing for jack, grouper, and conch. The women *soon go* to the conch salad stands, which means they are gathering onions, peppers, oranges, lemons, and limes. The conch will be cracked, taken out of its shell, sliced and diced upon order.

The island is the object extended from me (from us), because we see through one periphery. We (you and I—us) and the island, both object and perhaps subject, relying on the senses to keep us among the living. Lxxxx, freedom comes in the way we change the narrative, how we freeze and unfreeze the image, rearranging what we think we see into what we would like to or should see. What if the lens zooms in upon me in the cove, up from the reef, between the coconut trees, pen in hand, writing a letter? What if the lens readjusts a couple of degrees to the left, to the lone fisherman in the bay—the early worm getter? Lxxxx, although we are out of the lens, we are in the lens because we are attached to the island; it is part of (us) at this moment.

You do know you are part of (us), a collective? When waves inch their blue masses closer to the white sand, almost pleading to be acknowledged by the living, it is a shared experience. The waves, the breeze, the physical presentation of the island—what we interpret from sound and sight—are phenomena. And if we continue Kant's reasoning, then we understand that form only happens through phenomena. Form happens because of our need to give a feeling or situation context. One could say we were in form when we only viewed the island through one specific lens. We looked at the island, the island looked at (us). When I say (us), I mean the ones objectified, yet who seek distance from the daily objectification, always in runaway mode as contemporary art, but never running away. Only when we break form, meaning we switch point of view and rearranged narrative to create a new narrative, we are in the space where not only aesthetic freedom is possible, but beauty on our terms is realized.

Picture, and let (us) have a shared experience, a photo of my mother donning black *Get Christie Love* boots, offspring flanking her hips. For historical context, let's place her in the 1960s civil rights struggle, hence the Angela Davis 'fro and the silver hula-hoop earrings. She is the perfect icon for the '60s cultural revolution. The German philosopher Walter Benjamin would say that her photograph is a mechanical reproduction of an event, and furthermore he would insist, *Even the most perfect reproduction of a work of art is lacking in one element: its presence in time and space, its unique existence at the place where it happens to be.* Say my mother grew up understanding segregation and dynamite. Say the color of her skin mattered insomuch as skin color matters in America, and so she is a little defiant, yet, still mother. However, I would disagree with Benjamin in that, if we expand our concept of space, then time places itself in context.

Say to be in Nassau, coming from her Alabama background, growing up in a bootleg house complete with jukebox, might be considered revolutionary. The picture reveals our second visit to Nassau as a family. Each summer, my parents took my sister and me outside Alabama to help us know the expansive world. What the picture doesn't reveal is my longing to break free and explore the island. Even then, I understood I loved the unknown, the possibility of that yet to come. Water has held a fascination for me since I was four years old, crossing Lake Michigan from Detroit to Canada. My mother bought me a miniature red-and-yellow boat before the ride.

At four, I imagined anything to be possible and threw the boat in the water, fully expecting little boat to follow big boat to Canada. Never happened. Little boat sank to the bottom, but the water puzzled me, and I have always been drawn to it.

Along a parallel plane. The bearded man walking toward Coral Reef, hugging shoreline while wading in it, comes up to where I am contemplating aesthetic beauty, objects, and our relationship to phenomena, and takes a seat at the table next to me. I say that to say, we begin again at sundown. I fall asleep and awake to an unidentifiable rhythm—the electronic guitar fretted—pulsating against my window. The *thump* will not let me sleep, so I put my jeans on and follow the busted speakers' *thump*. The music is coming from Coral Reef, the place where I post up and write in the morning. The coral is hardest to negotiate, so I am careful. I have this theory that water carries certain memories through the particles it accrues over centuries, ions. Every time I pass the bay, I am listening for the echo of some distant memory.

DEAR Lxxxx, I have to tell you about last night while walking back from Coral Reef after eating crab claws, peas, and rice. For a moment I felt I could touch the ceiling of the universe, that maybe space wasn't so infinite. The sky looked like liquid tar, an opaque black mat. But there they were, two celestial stars charting an alternate imagination. I would like you to join me within this infinite space because what I found last night is that, though space is infinite, one's perception can alter the length of that space, even in its vastness, if only for a moment. We are meeting within the mind, of course, but nonetheless, a real connection.

Another day. Three dogs. Two sprawled on the white sand, the incoming foam washing over their pelts. The other dog, white with black patch over left eye, enjoys himself, stealing away in the azure. We already know memory creates imagistic metaphors that strengthen a primal scene. Through memory, we already had an afterimage of Coral Reef, which we explored in an earlier conversation. A subsequent visit reveals the (un)erased, which, if we were still working within the framework of Coral Reef, would strengthen the afterimage, thereby creating alternative variables that affect the senses within narrative. Upon further investigation, how could I have missed the flat to the right with conch shells lined around the white brick fence? The pink upturned shells are a perfect complement to the lavender.

Lxxxx, excuse me, but I was supposed to be your eyes. What

does it mean the fans are industrial and high velocity, or there are two television flat screens on perches? In the middle of the bar, there is an oil-on-linen painting hanging from the roof. The man in the picture is against the backdrop of Hatchet Bay. As a matter of fact, if I were in my villa by Hattie right now and opened the front door, this would be the image I saw, minus the man. So, now I have an afterimage and the man. There is a makeshift wooden stand, and the man is gutting a grouper, his John Henry forearms gleaming in the sun that hangs low over the bay.

Let us not forget the man we saw walking along the shore analogous to our time continuum (space), kicking a rotted coconut. This morning I saw him rise out of the sea like Poseidon. Then he turned back toward the sea, dove under a wave, came up, and wiped his face. The man was taking a morning bath, fully clothed, as if in the middle of a baptism. But hold on. If I wait one more day, I will discover that he has been walking in a daze ever since he came home and caught his wife in a state of infidelity. Then too, sitting with the sea day and night we come to learn each wave has its own afterimage. The tide rushes it in, and before it is gone, the voyeur will remember the wave's arcing position. Every time I remember the sea, it is filled with these afterimages, rushing in, moving away, a cat-and-mouse game between lovers who hunger for each other but cannot kiss for more than a second. An eternal infatuation where the love is *never-ending*.

This morning, the knock comes unexpected since Mateo and I said our goodbyes before he went to his construction job on Harbour Island. Opening the door, the slightly heavyset man who has his forefinger and thumb pointed like a gun squeezes the imaginary trigger and says, *Gotcha!* I'm trying to construct the man's facial features into someone recognizable, but I can't. Then I stare again, and the man's face focuses, and it's the same Haitian transplant with no shoes I met sitting on a giant turtle shell those many years ago in front of a small one-room house in Gregory Town. Franz Pantaleon had become a grown man, complete with receding hairline. We sit on the front steps of my apartment, enjoying the sunrise over the bay. Franz is still a cautious, guarded person. He tells me he never thought he would see me again. When I met Franz, he had an airplane, two cigarette boats, and a couple of fishing vessels. I never asked him how it all began, but sitting here now, with morning almost set and time perhaps inconsequential, I ask. Franz leans back a bit, like he's trying to remember.

The '80s were the opening to a gateway of drugs flowing from Columbia to the United States. Franz was sitting on the front steps of his house when a guy came walking two large dogs down the street. For some inexplicable reason, the man let go of the leash, and the dogs ran ahead and pounced on a pale man walking toward them. The man who let go of the leash kept walking past his attack dogs and then whistled. Getting up off the ground, the attacked man grabbed the biggest boulder he could find by the bush, ran, and hurled it, but coming down the street at that moment were the police, and the boulder smashed the side window of the police car.

The police had assumed the man was a drunk and wanted to take him to jail, except Franz came to his aide, explaining how the dogs and man that were now gone were the real culprits. The police let the pale man go, and Franz saw him again coming down the street the next day. This time his brother was on the steps with him and says, "That mon keep telling me he got connections in South America. You know people say he kinda loco." Franz ignored the loco part, hopped off the steps and caught up to him. After talking a while, they went to a phone booth.

Weeks later, Franz's brother was in Bogotá. What he found was a seventeen hundred square-foot warehouse with bricks of cocaine stacked to the ceiling. Shortly thereafter, Franz traveled down to Bogotá because he could fly an airplane and knew the route to Eleuthera; the Columbian pilots could only get the plane to San Carlos. The Columbians had a thousand kilos that needed to be moved to the states. Franz told them, "that's your problem not mine." In translation that meant, *If I transport these kilos, I get five hundred—bottom line. If the DEA catches me, they all belong to me.* Franz assumed the controls in San Carlos and made it to Haiti, the place of his birth, whose horseshoe mountain offered the gateway to Eleuthera. Once the plane glided low through the horseshoe, it would stay close to the water, under radar detection. Once Franz came up the left coast, he made out the curve from James Cistern leading to the cliff that forms the hatchet in Hatchet Bay. One thousand kilos wrapped in fiberglass were dropped in the water with his brother and a crew waiting in a boat. Franz, with the other two Columbian pilots in the cockpit, landed the plane in North Eleuthera. The customs officials cleared him and his guest. The rest, as they say, is history.

R

6

SAME SKY,
DIFFERENT WORLDS

DEAR RANDALL,

Randall, are you always complicated? I mean do you always say
a lot to explain something simple? Wait—maybe that's not right
either. I like it. I just always have to read it more than once to get it
right. I'm never sure about my first interpretation of your letters.
When I spoke to you the other night by phone, I only wanted to
be heard, especially in a place like this where each one of us ladies
often feels forgotten, nonexistent—voiceless. Do you know I fought
with Derrida's and Kant's theories for months before I understood
language will always fail because it cannot bring back the moment,
no matter how articulate the writer is—but in this instance, maybe
you are right. Interpretations will always be subjective, but at that
moment on the telephone, I wasn't expecting you to analyze my
problem. I only wanted you to listen and share some of my pains
and insecurities about being here in jail. I've learned that sometimes
we make mistakes that are so big, solutions don't come easily; some
things you can't control, like this situation. I have to go through the
fire.

I also wanted to write regarding the Eleuthera section and
how you got started in the drug trade. I knew after I read that piece
that the situation around my incarceration takes you back to a place
you probably disconnected from a long time ago, but at the same time
allows you to write down these memories. My being in this situation
and your sticking by me helps you heal a little because you know you
are giving me the support you lacked when you were in my shoes. I
also received the letter about your arrival and travels to the island. I
had to read it a few times just because I kept imagining myself there.

I'm glad you made it there safe and had a good time. It's
amazing how time changes everything, but certain things remain
the same. Eleuthera sounds amazing, and your description of it
resembles Puerto Rico in many ways. I could see the dark blue
water and the white sand. I could hear the sound of the ocean—its
movement like a slow dance with the wind, the waves curling on the
edge of the shore, white foam rising, trailing behind the current.
I know all you are doing is keeping my senses sharp, and at this
moment, I am living through you. I am definitely not here. You bring
truth to the statement: *freedom is a state of mind.*

Mateo sounds like a nice guy who may have a lot of
interesting stories to share with you about his pops. Daniel's wife
seems like an interesting character. I bet if her eyes could talk, you

would have a movie to write. Is the earth red? Did you get a little nervous when you walked through customs, or did this time around have a different feel? I bet you felt a little lighter because now you are there simply to enjoy all that you couldn't back then. I'm also working on some short stories, giving the characters a narrative of their own and then trying to find common themes that will intersect them together.

You once said, *How free am I?* I don't think any of us are free because there are too many things tying us down. When I say us, I mean every adult in the world. We all have our share of responsibilities. People can be imprisoned in so many different ways, not just physically, like me. I feel "free" when I live through my imagination and your reality. I think I am able to see what you're experiencing because my memories of the island of Puerto Rico are a reflection of what you are living. There are many differences between the islands, but in terms of the physical landscape, I think they are pretty much the same: breathtaking and beautiful. However, I am intrigued by its difference, the elements of Eleuthera that make it unique.

How did you know my favorite picture you sent is the one of you, your mom, and li'l sis in Nassau? I want you to know that with every scene you describe, you take me on a different journey. This three-dimensional trip of what you see and describe, to what I imagine and try to visualize of what actually is, shows how language can influence my perception. This time away from society and everyday obligations has put me in a time capsule. The world keeps moving; the clock's second hand keeps ticking, but it doesn't seem to matter as much as it did out there. When you're doing time, instead of letting the time do you, you try to make the most of every minute. You take advantage of the freedom from responsibilities and social constraints and indulge in "me time" to do what you want to do, what you always asked God to give you time to do: time to read, to get in tune with your spiritual side, to get in touch with yourself, to figure out what you really want to do with the rest of your life. Sometimes we need to be taken out of the real world to realize what we need to do when we get back out there. A lot of people don't ever get this opportunity. I may be leaving this place with another felony, but I'm also leaving with so much more.

Randall, in an attempt to understand the concept of time, we mirror it with life because we relate it to our own existence, but in reality, time is an illusion, a divine mystery. Time would not be important if we weren't forced to measure it. We are tortured with it and trained early not to waste it, but naturally we do the opposite. Upon self-reflection, we realize it isn't time we are wasting, it's our lives—the allotted space we are given here on earth. When we are young, we desire to be older, chasing freedom to do as we please. When we get older, we discern that children have the ultimate freedom in every sense—they exist solely to love and live. They are not bound by responsibilities, and their thoughts are not yet tainted or influenced by social constructions. Adults can only be mentally free. Time forces us to search for ways to defy the laws of physiology; we fear the unknown and yearn for immortality. Words and art become weapons and time a mark in His-Story. We become aware of the duality of it all. Life is a mirror of time monitored by two hands. Pay attention to the sound of it passing you by.

I woke up around 9:00 p.m. and went out to the rec deck to read your excerpts. I sat by the gate to feel a li'l breeze, and just as I began reading, the storm starts pouring. The rain came down so hard, I could feel the mist through the gate, the smell of dirt rising, lightning and thunder echoing brightly, dancing through the night sky. I hadn't seen rain come down like that in a long time, and I wondered if these were the same clouds with you in Eleuthera. We are under the same sky, though sometimes it feels like we are in two different worlds. I like your theory about water carrying certain memories through particles that accrue over time. I think there's a lot of truth to this, but I also believe you only scratched the surface. The earth is over 70 percent water. Can you imagine how much history is buried at the bottom of the ocean, how many stories lost at sea?

Ever wonder why they call it sea? Maybe because it's been around to witness everything since the beginning. It's such a living thing: it has its own distinct sound, color, movement, and senses. My grandmother used to tell my cousins and me the ocean was jealous, and we couldn't play with it because it would pull us in and swallow us. I think she used to say this to scare us—and it worked. At the start of every summer, our first trip to the beach always seemed like a ritual. Don't laugh, and don't think my family is into *brujeria*, because we are not, but she would get coconuts and chop off the top. We had to walk toward the ocean without spilling the water and pray, asking god to take away the negative things in our lives and bring us clarity. When the water level was deep enough for us to fall into, we would have to turn around, giving our backs to the water, pour the coconut water over our head, toss the shell behind us, then fall backwards asking the ocean to wash away the bad and bring us back up renewed. I don't know if this actually worked, but sometimes it made me feel lighter; does that makes any sense? I don't know, but it's one of my memories of the Caribbean that stands out.

My mother never participated in these practices, but she's not Puerto Rican; she's Salvadorian, and they practice religion differently—more Catholic-based. Seems like everything we discuss has a connecting thread. You never stop thinking about this idea, do you? You just keep building on it, or am I wrong? I can see the trip taking on a whole new meaning for you, and I'm glad I could be a part of it, even from a distance.

Today I was taken on an outside medical trip to New York Hospital. I got a CAT scan done, and they gave me an IV with a solution to dye my organs so they could see if there are any tears on my bladder or kidneys from the surgery I got done in Ecuador. Today was a beautiful day—the weather perfect, the sun shining, and traffic was light. We breezed through Brooklyn and Manhattan with ease and I was a li'l disappointed we didn't take longer to get to and from the hospital. I wore my favorite Khakis and my white on whites, and I put two fingertips of Vaseline behind my ears to keep my lips moist. This is how the girls hide the lip gloss; they put a little dab of Vaseline behind both ears because they don't allow us to take anything with us to court or anywhere outside the dorm. My hair has gotten really long, so I rocked a tight ponytail. The guards shackled my feet with cuffs that connected to a chain that wrapped around my waist, and they put handcuffs on me. They both wore bulletproof vests. I really felt like a criminal. When we walked into the hospital, people stared at me and moved away like I was dangerous. At first, I couldn't help but smile because I was so happy to be outside, to feel the heat of the sun on my skin, to inhale fresh air. God, I miss being free so much. I swear I even got butterflies in my stomach. The most embarrassing moment came when the director of the radiology department asked me for my name and shook my hand. He treated me like a human being, and that is so rare when you are in shackles. The polite gesture brought tears to my eyes, and when the male officer walked away, the female officer handed me some tissue and told me it would be okay.

I never imagined I would be in this situation again; it seems like a nightmare still. Somewhere along the line, I'm gonna wake up and this will all be over, but mistakes don't fade away easily. The officer tried to make small talk, but I didn't feel like sharing. I just remained quiet for the most part and enjoyed everything outside of what was happening to me. I even got to see myself in a real mirror—not the fun house mirrors they have in here, but a real mirror, and I look kind of fly despite being pale. I know with a li'l tan I'll be good to go. I still haven't heard anything new, but I remain hopeful. I will talk to you more about this matter another time. I need to tell you that ever since I got the journal you sent, I've been writing in it like crazy, trying to write all the things I want to remember. It's a lot different than regular paper because I feel like it's more personal. I've always had one. I'm in love with the little blue book, thanks again. I read this essay by Martin Luther King, Jr., titled "The Three Dimensions of a Complete Life," and I found it touching. He talks about the Book of Revelations and how John explains the three dimensions of a complete life, which are length (the push of a life forward to achieve its personal ends and ambitions), breadth (the outward concern for the welfare of others), and height (the upward reach for God). He says most people are never able to live a complete life because they get stuck either with personal struggles or with helping others, but rarely do they complete the triangle and include God or faith in their lifestyle. Most people seek the Divine when they are facing serious problems, when only a miracle can change their fate. This is my situation right now. All I do is pray, because I swear no human being can hear me or do shit to change my destiny.

I sit back and think about the people I helped when I was home, the relationships I had. None of those people are around now. No one looks out for my son, or even bothers to ask my mom how he's doing. There's no loyalty. People are only out for themselves. I sit back and reflect on all the time I wasted on fake friends and relationships. I wasted a decade and change on men who did nothing but weigh me down because I didn't know how to let go. I helped these two assholes raise kids that weren't mine, and now that mine is out there all alone, they can't even look out for my li'l boy. Not even on the strength I helped them with their kids when they were down. I was so stressed out when I was home over losing love, when all along love was sitting on my lap waiting for me to love him back. I realize now that everything has been taken away from me, that I placed value on things that weren't worth the effort. Did I ever tell you the story about Li'l Papa? Before I begin, I need to tell you that my son is my most beautiful creation. I love him more than anything in the world, and I regret nothing when it comes to how he came into being, even if it cost me a lot of heartache and pain.

After I graduated from SUNY Albany, I started dating this young guy Papote. He was no good, but he was wild and spontaneous, and I fell for him hard. When I got with him, his daughter was six months old, and I helped raise her. We stayed together for three and a half years, and the beginning was a lot easier than the rest of it. See, when I first met Papote, he was on leave from his job as a bridge painter, waiting to be called back. He was flipping a few grams here and there, drove a nice car, and the loving truly had me sprung. Papote wasn't stable, though. He was a stickup kid and was on the run for a while. I let him move upstate with me. He couldn't work legit, so he sold grams of coke or crack here and there. The responsibilities really fell on me because his hustle wasn't consistent; one minute the work was good, the next minute the work was trash, his connects weren't reliable. I worked two jobs to support us.

I got pregnant quick. Papote wanted a family, and I wanted to make him happy. The pregnancy was hard because I worked all the time. We argued a lot, and he ended up leaving and going back to New York City. Now I was pregnant, working, alone, and still taking care of him. I didn't want to abandon him and let him down. He was on the run because he'd robbed somebody to help support me. I kept feeling sorry for him and his daughter.

The day I went to find out the sex of the baby, I discovered the baby's limbs were bowed, and the extremities were not developing at a normal rate. She or he was two months behind, and the head was bigger than the body. The doctor wanted me to undergo further testing. I was sent to another doctor in the county who then referred me to a genetic specialist at Columbia Presbyterian in Manhattan. I was six months when I found out the baby did not have kidneys, that there was a hole in the cerebellum, and that the baby would not survive past delivery. The doctors told me I would be risking my life if I tried to carry the baby to full term and that I should have an abortion. The procedure took two days. Papote went through it all with me, and we cried together. He had started working again and left his job to accompany me through the procedure. He took care of me, and I was lost, I didn't even speak for days at a time.

The first day of the procedure I went to get the sticks put in to dilate the cervix, and it was painful. I remember like it was yesterday. I was on the table and the doctor had me open my legs wide and scoot down to the end. He placed a metal contraption to keep me open and began to insert the sticks. I started screaming and holding Papote's hand tight, squeezing it with all my might, and the pressure continued and just became more intense. The doctor kept telling me to be still because he could hurt me. But I couldn't stop shaking. Then Papote did the unexpected and laid his head on my chest. He looked at me and said, *I'm here, you not alone; we going through it together. Breathe and relax, it will be over soon. You're so strong.* I inhaled deep with tears running down the sides of my face, and I stared into his honey-colored eyes and let the pain numb me.

The second part of the procedure was scheduled for the following morning. Papote took me home and got me the pain medication the doctor prescribed. I could feel myself gradually opening up. My walls were expanding and the pressure was intense. I got high for the rest of the day until I passed out. The next morning we drove to Albany Medical and I put on the paper gown. Papote and I said a prayer for the baby. We asked the doctor if he could stop the baby's heart before the procedure. The doctor asked if I would donate the remains to a genetic testing center in California. He said they would give me the answers I was looking for.

Those bastards wrote me a letter four months later telling me the baby was not a dwarf and that the genetic mutation was a one-in-a-million situation. I was messed up behind that news. I felt like I couldn't produce a normal child, like there was something wrong with me. My relationship with Papote was super fucked up by that point. Something died between us. His sister ended up telling me he was still sleeping with his baby's mom. I broke up with him a week later. I slept with another man and enjoyed it.

I went to Puerto Rico to bust a move and clear my head. The same day I got there, I fainted and ended up getting seven stitches on my chin. That's when I found out I was pregnant. When I got back to New York, I told Papote, and we got back together. My pregnancy was tough. I wasn't working and he wasn't either. We were not getting along. He was treating me fucked-up. I didn't have my car because my plates were suspended for three months, so I couldn't make any money. I also developed placenta previa and kept hemorrhaging every time I was on my feet for too long. I ended up in the hospital twice. I was bleeding chunks that looked like pieces of liver. Eventually the placenta moved, and I was fine. My baby was fighting the whole time to be with me.

The day I went into labor, Papote and I were not together. We had had a big fight and had broken up. I called him and told him the baby was coming. He came over and stayed with me until we went to the hospital. They sent me home because I wasn't ready.

Papote's grandmother lived a block away from the hospital, so we walked to her house, and he let me sit in her tub. He rubbed my back and just helped me with everything. My parents were around the first day, but then both of them had to go to work. Papote's family stayed with me and gave me all the support in the world. I was in labor for thirty-eight hours.

Papote was the first person to see my son enter this world. He cut his umbilical cord. He cried for forty-five minutes and prayed.

Wait—let me backtrack. Actually, as soon as the baby came out, before the cord was cut, I pulled him up to my chest and held him. He was born sunny side up, facing me. After we connected, the doctor held him, and Papote cut the cord, and then I breastfed him. I remember saying, *I did it*, and Papote greeted him and said, *Hi Papa.* Ever since that moment I have called my son Papa!

Papote ended up telling me later that he had had a threesome with two girls. At that point I was hurt, but I was more into my son, whom I named Isaías. They said my placenta was hot because I had a fever so they decided to keep Isaías in the NICU. He couldn't be with me. I was only allowed to feed him. This bothered me at first, but I was in so much pain that I just wanted to rest before I dealt with the baby. Papote asked me for a second chance. He loved the baby and me. I asked him to take a DNA test before he signed the papers for the birth certificate, but he didn't want to. He wanted to sign without the test; he trusted me.

His mother, on the other hand, started talking shit about the baby, saying my son was too dark to be part of Papote's family. She secretly went and bought two DNA test for both Layla, Papote's daughter, and my son. I didn't feel offended, though, when Papote told me, and I agreed to go with him and the kids to get tested. His daughter was really close to me, and somehow she knew what was going on. She cried and kept hitting the doctor, saying, *Don't touch my brother, that's my brother.* Papote had to grab her and take her to the other room, and she was screaming, *Leave my brother alone.*

Layla didn't calm down until I came over and held her in my arms. After that, we went back home and chilled. I was overwhelmed because Papote wasn't much help around the house, but I was happy because we were together as a family. We were both unemployed, but I was doing a few moves to make money as well as receiving food stamps and WIC for the baby. Christmas was coming, and we were so broke. I didn't want to have a bad one, so I went up to my storage and found some grams of coke I had stashed. We got rid of it, and the kids had a really great Christmas.

The day before Papote's birthday, his sister Jezebel called and told me the results. She said Layla was his, but my son wasn't. I had to contain myself because Papote was in the living room with the baby. I couldn't believe this was happening. I knew I had slept with one other man, but we'd used protection. How could this be? I thanked her and asked her not to blow it up until the results were given to him at the clinic.

The next day was Papote's birthday, and we had a real nice time. We had a few friends over. I made him a cake, and we drank and took mad pictures. The next day the clinic called saying the results were in. I drove Papote to the front of the building and told him that the baby and I would wait for him outside. As soon as he entered the building, I blew it with my son. I was scared. I didn't want him to hurt the baby or me. I needed to protect the baby. When he called me asking where I had gone, I told him he needed to be alone. He was in shock and broken, his manhood tossed somewhere his eyes couldn't reach.

I fucked Papote up bad, and I didn't mean to. He needed closure. He said he needed to see us, but I was afraid. Eight days later, I gave in, and by this time, everyone knew. I let him come and see us, and we cried and he asked me why. I told him, "I went looking for comfort in the arms of another man because I was heartbroken. I didn't really want him, but I wanted to feel appreciated. You fucked with my womanhood."

Papote wanted to know who the man was, but I had no way of contacting him. His old number was disconnected, and the mutual friends we had didn't know his whereabouts. It wasn't like I was going to tell him anyway. Papote's mother took him to a clinic to get tested for sexually transmitted diseases. There, he met a girl named Audi. Not even a week had passed when he had slept with and impregnated her. She is now the mother of his son Christian, born November 2010.

Still, Papote continued to come around for three months. He came to use me, and I let him. I missed him. I wanted him back. I would make him breakfast when he came to my house. He would ask me to get rid of whatever bundles of H he had, and I would. We'd have sex, but he wouldn't kiss me. He would take the money I made for him and spend it on the new girl. Layla and I still spent time together, and that meant a lot to me. I had been in her life since she was six months old. She was like my daughter too. One day he asked me to drop her off at her mother's house, and I agreed. We dropped her off, and turns out it was Layla's mother's birthday. Papote came back to my car talking about how pretty this bitch look, and that shit pissed me off. I was so jealous. I flipped on him and asked, "Why the fuck didn't you stay with her instead of taking me serious?" His response was simple: "Bitch, you got the nerve to talk shit, and you the reason we not together." But I knew better. I knew he stood with me because I made moves for him and kept his pockets right without him having to risk himself.

I was that bitch that did it all, and it was convenient. His women were used to lying on their backs and receiving. I was never the type to expect shit to come to me. I went out and made it happen by any means necessary. I knew the deal from the start; that's why I would do the things I did. Papote would give me the soft and expect the bread for it. But I would flip it by making it hard and double the money and not tell him shit. He thought all along he was using me, but I was shortchanging that dude like crazy. In the end, he found out because he tried to embarrass me one day and I had to shut him down. I would cook up cocaine for my connects, and the extras we would keep and move. It wasn't much, but we survived. I paid rent and all our expenses, and we got high every day. There wasn't money to burn, but we weren't borrowing money to survive, either. It would have been easier if we didn't have habits, but we were both addicts.

During my pregnancy, I think I hustled the most. I was movin' bud by the pounds. I didn't do breakdowns, so I would only see a few hundred off every move. But I did it. Papote started messing with heroin and didn't know what the fuck he was doing, and if I hadn't schooled him, he probably would've gotten killed trying to serve customers bundles of crushed up pills whenever the work went bad. This dude was a straight parasite. Everything he touched he destroyed. That's why I would make the moves myself, to keep the flow light and consistent. I would include him, but kept him away from people that mattered, you know? Cause they would do him dirty if they suspected any funny business. My way of handling shit intimidated him, and he would get mad, try to hit and rob me. I was so fucking stupid. I still wanted to believe he was the father of my child so, right or wrong, I would always come back to him and fix everything he fucked up.

Anyway, the day I had an argument with him about his baby's mom, he said he was happy he never bought my son anything. I pulled over and kicked him out of my car. He tried to steal my purse, but the cops were parked a few cars in front of us, and I threatened to call them. I took my purse out of his hands, tossed him a dollar bill and six quarters and said, "get the fuck out of my car." We didn't speak for months.

When my grandmother died, I called him because I still had not received the new birth certificate with the name change, and I needed a notarized document giving me permission to travel internationally with Isaías. He wanted to include all this extra shit about not being the biological father, but I asked him not to embarrass me. That I had gone through enough. He calmed down and told me to come get it. I took Isaías with me. When Papote approached the car I was on the phone, and he laid the envelope on the passenger seat and played with Isaías through the window. I asked him to wait, but he told me he couldn't, that he still wasn't over it. By this time, he had already moved on to a new girl, and that she was pregnant, too.

I didn't speak to Papote again until November 2011. He was surprised to hear from me, said he heard I was in jail but couldn't believe it. I told him I was thinking of him and Layla. And he asked about Isaías. He said he worried about him, but didn't offer any help with my son.

A part of me still feels like Papote is the father because we went through everything together. He's the reason I went through with the pregnancy. I wanted to have a family with him. Looking back, it seems that he just wanted a family. His sister said I fucked him up, and that's why he started having kids with different girls, but I didn't believe that shit. He told me about his newborn, Elizabeth, and his son, Christian, and how Audi had been a rebound, that he'd never loved her. He used her to get over me. He was working and doing real good now. I was happy for Papote. He was being a man— something he couldn't be with me. At first it bothered me, but that's life, and I don't regret my son. He's perfect. Papote told me he missed me, and I asked if he forgave me, and he said he'd forgiven me a while ago. He had moved on but was sorry things turned out the way they did for me. I cried because I wished he had stayed with my son and me. He asked me to stay in touch, and I called him twice after that, but no more. I'm at peace knowing he still thinks of me, knowing the woman he is with could never walk in my shoes. He's taking care of her, but I took care of him and Layla. He remembers, and I know someday I will see him again.

I know my son missed out on a good father. Maybe I will fall in love again someday. I'll fall in love again, and the man I choose will be an even a better father to my son.

Did I ever tell you how I found Isaías' father? About a month after Papote and I broke up, I looked into my old phone and started searching for his number and our mutual friends. I dialed every number and couldn't find this dude. Then I remembered my last text to him. I'd sent it while I was in Puerto Rico after I found out I was pregnant. I told him I was getting back with my old man, and that I wasn't gonna call him anymore 'cause I was pregnant. His wife texted me back from her cell asking me who I was pregnant from. I never answered, but I kept the number. When I couldn't get in touch with him, I called her and asked for him. She thought I was from the probation office—feds, turns out. He called me like two minutes after I spoke to her. I told him who I was and that we have a child together.

I let him know off top I didn't want to blow up his spot with his wife. I also asked why he didn't tell me he was married. He said, "I knew I was gonna see you again." I was furious because I felt like he did it on purpose to fuck me over. I promised him I wouldn't tell his wife anything, but he had to be a man and own up to his. He let me know that, a week after we slept together, he got arrested for conspiracy with the Trinitarios, a Dominican gang in Washington Heights, and now he was out on house arrest with an ankle bracelet. I would talk to him over the phone. I even gave him a cell phone when his broke. We would Skype chat. We exchanged pics on Facebook, but I ended up deleting his ass. I would go see him randomly, and he would always try to kiss and feel me up. I wouldn't let him rock, but I would keep it cool with him so when the day came he would recognize the baby.

A few days after I came back from Ecuador, I spoke to him and he got sentenced to probation. He asked me for a loan, and I told him we would have to discuss it when he came to meet the baby. The bastard never came, and I got arrested days later. I was hurt he didn't bother to come meet his son, but what did I expect? He don't love me or the baby. He doesn't even know me like that. I haven't tried to contact him, and I do want to, but not now—when I get out. He has four other daughters, but my son is his only boy, and the only light-skinned one. That's probably why he doubts the baby is his. But I want him to take a DNA test—not because I want money from him. I don't. I don't even want to change my son's last name. I only want to fix the name of the father on the birth certificate. Sometimes I tell myself to forget about it, but I know my son is going to ask about him someday, and I will have to explain. What if I get killed because some shit from my past catches up with me and my son grows up thinking Papote is his father and looks for him and asks him? Then I'm going to look like a fucking liar to my son, and I don't want that. I want those papers fixed, and I want him to know his sisters and dad. Even if they don't want nothing to do with him—at least to let them meet. Am I stupid for wanting that for my boy? Do you think I should walk away and think of some bullshit lie to tell my son? I have to be real with him. That's why I gotta fix this when I get out.

Lxxxx

7

FLIPPING THE SCRIPT

DEAR LXXXX,

Perhaps I am that complicated, and I'm sorry, but Papote will never be in your son's life like you want. If that's what you want, then that's what I want, but the way he thinking as a man right now will not allow him to get past his feelings. It takes an incredibly strong man to be down with that situation. I understand the connection between you and Papote and Isaías, but everything you have revealed tells me he won't—or better yet, perhaps he can't. My brother Reginald got this saying: *love is what love does. If love ain't treating you right, then you need to find a new love.* You were mistreated, and don't downplay that. I know because I have been a version of Papote in some form or another, and I am certain he wanted to use you and play off of your love because he could. He discovered your weakness and guilt and took advantage of your feelings.

Maybe Papote has his own history to make. People can change if they want to. Love blinds us all, yet we all want to be loved blindly. I said before in one of my earlier letters, you have answered every question you ever wanted to know about your life and relationship with men and love. The answers are in the words.

Lxxxx, I know I did some fucked-up shit I'm not proud of in my life. I love that you don't give me passes. In one of your letters you wrote: *I wonder what drove you to use women this way, and I wonder if you were tellin' the truth when you told me before that you harbored a lot of guilt about the things you did to women back in those days. You sound like you caught in between feelings when it comes to that pimp shit, like sometimes you proud and sometimes you not, and I can dig that.*

My situation was more predicated on being involved in the drug scene—not going out looking for women to purposely fuck up their lives, but nonetheless, I did. Their names were Jo-Jo, Punkin, and Pepper, women who sold their bodies before I met them because they were addicted to crack.

Pepper was little different in that our relationship was one based more on mutual respect, meaning, it wasn't very sexual or intimate at all, but we loved each other in that twisted street way. If I would have ever hit that girl, she would have killed me—she was just that deadly. I didn't abuse them in that way.

When Jo-Jo and I fought, it wasn't about going out on the track to make money. It was more of a jealousy thing with her. I mean, she sold pussy a hundred miles an hour out of both pant legs and expected me to stay monogamous. However, I understand

I am as guilty as if I did hit them and blacken their eyes because I contributed to their degradation and my own.

Lxxxx, how can I ever bring up the fact I walked the streets with prostitutes, that at times my survival depended on a woman selling her body for me? We robbed johns to feed our cocaine habit, to survive. I understand there are no words to articulate the shame and guilt I walk with everyday. It is only through writing this memoir that I am able to own up to my past. You see, memoir is about (re)memory, about reliving events, deconstructing those events, finding epiphanies, if possible, all while staying true to the narrative(s). Writing this memoir is difficult. I have to go back to spaces I tried to bury long ago. It's all the *digging* that drains you, Lxxxx. And when you are through *digging*, you have to wallow in it before you let it go. It's the "it" that kills you. But then I have to edit. And so I relive it, again and again.

Lxxxx, every day I live with an incorrigible past. I don't wear the things I tell you like a badge of honor. Really, my past is shameful. And when I talk to women, it is something that perhaps I will never bring up. I trust you, so you get this, in this way, uncut and raw. I mean, sure, I'm writing a memoir and telling dirty secrets, but I am scared to death of how people will view me once it's out. That's real. But I know I have to tell this story in order to continue freeing myself of the guilt. That is why I write it. I mean, I could just never tap those memories, but they will not stop echoing in my head, so I conjure them and write to get free. Love, or the need to love, or the need to be loved is a terrible jones, and we all be ill'n for a fix of the good stuff—a beloved body.

I had a beloved body once, but I lost it to what I could not recognize. Her name was Natalie Denise Thompson. She stood six feet in sandals and acted as my immediate supervisor at a document coding company in DC. After the embezzlement at the bank, I found myself back in DC with a temp job as a document coder, a year before I would get the telecommunications job. The firm had been awarded a big contract to index all of the legal documents pertaining to why the space shuttle Challenger blew up. My group had been assigned documents dealing with the O-Rings, which we now know to be the cause of that tragedy.

One day Natalie and I found ourselves going out after work for happy hour. I could tell she had been digging me by the way she called me to her desk to inquire how the work was coming, and if I had any questions about the current assignment. It became subtle flirtation. The next week I found myself in her apartment.

Natalie showered me with affection and love. She cooked dinner every night and wanted to show me what having a good woman can do for a hardheaded brother. I say that to say, I was too young to feel that kind of love. I had no room for another person. People could love me, but I could not love them back. Natalie brought me flowers every Friday because she wanted me to feel like I mattered in this world. She taught me about special moments, like walking in the snow on K Street during rush hour. Sadly, it would be years later, after a succession of women who could never measure up to her, that I would come to understand the phrase *you never miss the water 'til the well runs dry.*

All I had to do was drink the water, to believe in the replenishment of love. There is a scene in the play *Fences* by August Wilson in which Troy, who is the main character, is told by Rose that if he ain't trying to get with it, then he needs to step aside for the dude who is. Every time I read your letters, I see a young lady who's got more love than the universe got black space. Make sure you get some back. The thing is, if we flipped the script, inverted the narrative, and placed me where your history begins, I can tell you that I have always wanted to love, to be loved. The month before I met you on that New Years Eve, my sister and I had just celebrated my parents' fiftieth anniversary. What I'm saying is that a man and a woman found a way to love for fifty years. For fifty years they have found a way to stay in love, and perhaps "trying to stay in love" is the greatest love of all. I watched this love as a child and figured everyone had the capability to love as my mom and dad, so in many ways I have been chasing that model most of my adult life.

I will say the one constant motif in your narrative is love or wanting to be loved. It's funny because men think women have the choice of who they want to be with, and can better dictate their love lives. But I know now this to be false. Women fall victim to the same land mines of love that men do. There ain't no easy formula on how to love or how to be loved for anyone. Who to let in? Who not to let in? I would never have guessed you were going through these kinds of relationship problems with men. I would have said you too fine for those kinds of problems. But that's just some male ignorance talking. My own loves over the years have been dysfunctional, and I know I could have avoided all the madness, but Lxxxx, we can't help who we love. When we find the *good*, we try to hold on, as if that *good* will never come again if we let go.

The funny thing is that you cannot save people from the histories they are destined to make. Meaning, we can't stop life from beating us up. I know you and Papote fought. I know he hit you (even once is too much), and you perhaps forgave him because you loved him. But you did not love yourself in the process. Everybody was getting love but Lxxxx, who had to fight for love while loving everybody. I say this because I have been there, and I have been in those relationships where I'm fighting for the love I want and need while trying to figure out how to be a man, which is no good for either party. Perhaps I am trying to deal with my own guilt with women. Unhealthy relationships always reveal themselves in the end.

R

JOURNAL NOTE TO [SELF]:
A TALE OF TIME

The Atlantic always lingering—(in) the primal scene. Houses and buildings squeezed together as if this were the last plot of land on earth—a colonial district of early American homes, an architectural wonder weathering time. Telephone poles brace black electric wire, adding an aesthetic response to the mechanizations of the city. Narrow streets and sporadic hills diagram a landscape never too far from the ocean, while aureate, auburn, and gray accentuate the blue's backdrop. Layer upon layer, this system was destined to create exploration, pushing past the known limits for the sake of freedom. The rocks along the cliffs are black shale, sandstone morphed into slate. Haggard branches point toward each other from opposite sides of the street at the yellow sign, which reads: CAUTION.

EXCERPT III: ALL IN——

1993 to 1996 —— DC & MARYLAND

MAIL CALL: LXXXX PXXXX
INMATE NUMBER (37XXXXXX)
FEDERAL DETENTION CENTER
PO BOX 329002
BROOKLYN, NY 11232

JO-JO, PUNKIN, AND ME, 1993

Not three by three. Not two by two. It happens one by one. Every tangible item I thought mattered up until the time I was thirty-two years of age slowly slipped out of sight. Friends are always the first to disassociate themselves because they were never really friends, merely hangers-on for the good-time ride. The first ones out of the rented limo. Expensive menu-orderers, and they ain't got two pesos to rub together. Chrissy, the girl I'd thought I would marry, had packed her bags after all her signs were ignored, and so she disappeared into the three million people that make up DC with clothes, jewelry, artwork, and a strangled heart.

This can't last forever. She took the Laura Fields oil painting on linen and the ceramic comedy and tragedy faces that occupied the living room wall. Neither the tan wood-grain Samurai nor the black-on-black Porsche 944 were parked in front of the condo in Alexandria off Duke Street any longer. The savings account, the money under the mattress and in the safe house in King Street, and, finally, the condo—all gone. It's like I had never counted money in a money machine or taken skiing trips to Seven Springs in Pennsylvania. It's like I'd never closed down the bar or gone on shopping sprees with beautiful women digging in my pockets. I almost started to believe I had lived a fantasy. One day I found myself standing on 13th and P, holding a suitcase.

But her name was Jo-Jo. An amalgam of black and white hinting at Latina, when she said *'migo,* men wanted her to be Spanish. Spanish-speaking guys fell in love with her seven days a week, and sometimes eight. Her eyes were rain black, and she saved me. Many would have considered her a transportation mule, as she became skillful in passing through customs when I first began to travel to Eleuthera. She was nineteen when I met her. I had the cars, the money, and the cockiness. Could I be the hero that her father was not? That was what she wanted. *How do you say I'm sorry to a memory?* Call her a ride or die chick. She had the type of beauty that commands the blind to see—right now, and if you kissed her, you would think her lips were able to heal the world. Call her hood and down-wit-it because she came from up under poverty in a run-down row house on 13th and T. Five siblings and not one earned high school diploma. The white mother prostituted for years after arriving on 14th Street from the hills of West Virginia. The black father worked sporadically, which was a complicated feat since he lived in the bottle. They called him the head of the house.

For two years after my last drug trip to Eleuthera, I straddled between sane and insane. I lost my ambition, my drive to smuggle, to create money, but more than anything, I lost faith in people I called my friends. So I fell into the bottom of a glass stem. On the way down, no one offered me a hand to climb back up the rung of the ladder from which I descended. I was caught in a darkness.

There really was nowhere to go when the proprietor of the tourist home put me out because I could no longer pay the weekly rent. The first night I stayed in an abandoned car. The next morning Jo-Jo walked the eight blocks down from her house and we went over to 16th and S. She could tell I was defeated, and had never seen me that way before. I was older, more mature, made her laugh, told her things no one else had about her beauty and her self. No one ever asked to *know* her, and I did.

I waited for Jo-Jo across the street in a small circular park with two wooden benches and a swing set. Cars rode up and down the street, oblivious to me and my homelessness. Thirty minutes later Jo-Jo came out of the apartment building, walked across the street to where I was sitting and slid me five twenty-dollar bills.

One night after dating a trick, Jo-Jo came back to my rented room on Logan Circle with three hundred dollars. "There's more," she said, and we doubled back to the row house in Columbia Heights and eased around to the side of the building adjacent to an alley. Jo-Jo got on my shoulders and I hoisted her to the first floor apartment's window ledge, which she had left open before leaving. One upward thrust and she was inside. Through the living room she tiptoed until she reached the couch where the seventy-year-old man slept, knocked out from orgasm and vodka. Out of his back pocket Jo-Jo pulled the brown leather wallet and found her way to the door before I came back around the front. *The girl was stealth.* Jo-Jo taught me about surviving in the streets where everybody's taught not to giva fuck. *Body unraveling at the hemline, and the city cracks you. Everyday a hazard waiting to happen. Police be a reminder 911 right here, right now.* I had to transform myself from the person my mother and father raised me to be into a coldhearted muthafucka.

The drugs had me walking in a perforated daze. Like walking over cobblestone—but not really walking. Day no better than night. Love not love. Jo-Jo went willingly into the dissipating midnight snow, the torrential downpour in April, the yellow scorch of August, Christmas Day. And of course, her father hated me, considered me the number one reason his daughter was out in them cold streets. He didn't know she was living this life before I met her. *I could not save what was already lost.* Jo-Jo and her father showed love by fighting fisticuff style on the front stoop—him dragging her hair, her clawing and scratching until the police came. Call her wild thang, but it was a different kind of love, in that she wanted a father. *I could not be her father.* I could save her from the rapist wanting to take her body not of her free will. I could hover over and protect her from the streets. *But I could not save her.* The city had me struggling daily to survive the madness, and my red-boot walker of intrigue whistled to the johns and tricks in the alleyways because she loved me. But I didn't know how to even try because, sadly, I could not save myself.

I went through two years of living from shelter to shelter, sometimes on Lincoln Road, sometimes at the Mission on 14th and R, sometimes on South Capital Street. Whatever shelter I chose to stay in, the rules and regulations were always the same: check in at 6:00 p.m., check out at 6:00 a.m. Some would let you shower if you were lucky, and sleep on an army cot, but you had to be out by dawn, no matter the weather. If you missed the check-in, then the city was your home for the night.

During that last year, I reconnected with a DC dealer named Roscoe who took a chance on me because I had dealt with him when I was moving weight a few years prior. Before I could begin to sell the drug, Jo-Jo and I checked into a tourist home on Logan Circle to bag up the product. However, we ended up smoking everything in a span of two days because *the rock is holy.* I could not tell Roscoe the product had disappeared into vapors. He was unpredictable.

Squeezing the trigger of a gun was not problematic for him. Rather than take a chance on my life, I evaporated from the radius of his reach to Atlanta because it was close to Birmingham, and my father would help me get on my feet. Jo-Jo had two daughters to take care of and couldn't come with me, so I knew this would be our goodbye.

Within the first month of being in Atlanta, I got a job as an inventory clerk and rented an apartment with the help of my father, who believed me when I said I was trying to turn a new page. The Honda Accord I drove, my father helped secure with a promise that I would pay.

Within one year, I lost the car, the apartment, the job, and my self-worth all over again because I began smoking crack, wallowing in my failures. When my father put me on a bus back to DC, I told him I was going to make it this time, that I needed to succeed there in order to move on with my life. In return, he said he would never give up on me, but I could sense the disappointment behind the affirmation. When I arrived, I went to a homeless shelter in Virginia that allowed you to stay for six months if you found a job. I eventually secured my old telecommunications job in Pentagon City because I had left them on good terms. I then saved money, rented another apartment, and squared up my debt with the man I owed so I could live without watching my back.

After my return to DC, I went looking for Jo-Jo; however, when I knocked on her door on T Street, Jo-Jo informed me that she had started seeing a dude name Prophet, who was super jealous of me. Jo-Jo asked me to stay away because Prophet was violent and had killed people. So I did. Three months later, I met Punkin in a crack house on 13th Street between S and T. Punkin sold her body and cocaine concurrently, injecting as much effort into one as she did the other. It was often difficult to make clear distinctions as to which vice radiated more in her. Punkin walked confident with her sculpted-by-God Tina Turner legs, each stride exquisite. Whether or not one actually believed in God was inconsequential. To see those legs underneath a miniskirt strolling Logan Circle was to recognize a power greater than oneself. Her hip-switch compelled do-good men to screech their car tires and find fifty or sixty dollars for Punkin to perform magic.

She would prop those caramel legs on an abandoned stoop and serve crack to the hookers, the homeless, and the woebegone. She handled each customer differently because she understood the need to feed the body, the guttural hunger that craved a swirl of pallid smoke through a straight shooter. Punkin studied her customers before taking their money. She would reach into her plastic bag to pick out the appropriate amount of narcotic that fit her evaluation of the addict before her. One might need an oversized bag, stuffed heavy-handed, but nonetheless still only a dime bag in cost. Another addict might be a geek monster, playing and breaking every code of the streets, like selling their children's WIC vouchers or robbing old ladies—that addict would receive a skimpy bag. There were many more codes Punkin lived by that would never appear in an official document to be reviewed and studied.

Punkin became my woman on a night I made her feel something other than what it meant to be a streetwalker. We found each other in a crack house filled with sunken eye sockets, skin falling off bones, and the indescribable smell of human waste. It doesn't matter if I tell you which house because they are all the same. Fiends banging on the wrought iron gate, which is double-locked and has to be doubly unlocked to facilitate the traffic flow. Little or no furniture, maybe a mattress for people to sex, fuck, make love, or whatever happens when nakedness rubs together. Lighters flicking, glass stems swirling with smoke, and girls offering oral sex for a pull off of the pipe—sometimes guys offering this too. They are all the same. I found Punkin in one of these rooms in deep concentration. When she saw me, something clicked, like she was looking for someone to help her. Punkin and I formed a union that night on 13th and T Street. I took her home with me, bathed her, fed her, and after a couple of days, fucked her again with the love I knew I would never be able to fully give. To say she was my main woman meant I understood she would sell her body of her own free will, yet, by the same token, she understood I would hold the money, watch her back, and occasionally hit a sucker over the head and empty his pockets of the money from the two-week check he had just cashed at the corner liquor store. To reach this kind of understanding in a relationship meant that everything I had learned about treating women—everything I had learned about how to love—was gone, had vacated.

Punkin chased sparkling hubcaps down 13th on summer nights dressed in two-piece spaghetti-strap bras and matching thongs under white stretch pants. She hopped in cars with sunroofs, drop tops, or just plain metal buckets, only to veer quickly into an alley, slide a condom over the penis, and sexually perform for ten to fifteen minutes—or maybe clip a wallet and deplete the front pockets when the john orgasmed. When Punkin advertised and marketed her body, I walked a grid of four to five blocks, using T Street as our base and rendezvous point. Our internal clocks synchronized to bring us together in front of the Whitelaw, which back in its heyday had all the great jazz musicians perform and stay there. Now, the music that circled this building came from heel-clicking women whistling to johns or the homeless who owned this area at night, and people like me: men trying to make ends meet until the big payday came along, using any and everybody. We made our own drumbeats, blared our own trumpets, daring the police to stop the Charlie Parker soundtrack playing in our heads. I felt at home amid the five o'clock-shadowed men hugged against redbrick walls with heroin dragging them into a slow nod, the brims of their hats slicing their faces into half moons. And yet the undeniable desire to fly over the blue Caribbean into Hatchet Bay and smell its salted sea! To ride in a fishing boat undetected by the Coast Guard. I wanted to do it again.

"So, you expect me to believe you smuggled cocaine. Why should I believe you? I believe you made that shit up."

"What do you mean?" Actually, I understood. I also found it hard to believe I had fallen so low. In the two years we had been together, that part of my life had been suppressed by trying to make it to work on time in Pentagon City while chasing behind Punkin at night in DC. Any money we made, plus my paycheck, we spent right back on drugs. Craig was in Miami dealing with hard times and kept telling me to hold on. When you go from paying one hundred ninety-seven dollars for twenty-eight grams in Eleuthera to buying 3.5 grams for one seventy-five while still feeding a cocaine habit, failure is just around the corner. Many nights it was: Place pebble in stem. Sizzle then fall into a ravine. Cage the outside world. *The Last One.* But there is never a *last one.* Every night we smoked until not even the crumbs were left because *the rock is holy.*

"I mean we sleeping in a damn car. Wake up—we live in a bucket." Again, correct, but I could blame it all on Punkin—getting put out because she couldn't stop smoking crack in the basement apartment, coupled with the fact we argued every five minutes. Then I quit my telecommunications job before I got fired. We had been living in the car for a week. "So if you such a big shot, why don't you get us out of this damn car? Go smuggle some cocaine and do that. Better yet, stay right here while I sell my ass to get us out of this shit."

How do you respond to a painful truth and make your body disappear in an eye blink? Punkin knew how to remind me that yesterday's score doesn't win today's game. I was using history to pull myself out of a self-induced funk, a history that didn't mean anything to people who stood in the soup lines and slept with me in homeless shelters. I represented the failure that they could not escape themselves, yet in some way, I wanted to be better than they were. Night's solitude makes you contemplate these transgressions, like sleeping in a car where, only a block away, the slow *hum* of traffic comes from cars going to a destination, and you feel like the twisted streetlamp on the corner is shining—is spotlighting you—to inform the world: *here lies failure.* The men and women passing on the sidewalk, laughing about the good times, had homes to slide a door key into. I had a metal bucket and Punkin. She didn't return to our makeshift home that night, and I knew she was selling her body for herself, getting high for herself—it was always about the self.

Fed up with depending on a woman for my survival, I decided to leave the metal bucket we had lived in for a week on 13th and S. I then crisscrossed over to Rhode Island Avenue against the grain of rush hour traffic to my old friend Fat Joe's house to shower and change clothes. My clothes were being stored there after the eviction from my basement apartment in Springfield. When Fat Joe opened the door and greeted me with his disappointed look, as if he really didn't want to let me in, I could feel the filth—not only on my body, but also in my bones. I wanted to tell Fat Joe that being in these streets was like being stuck in a landscape where everybody was moving forward except me. Fat Joe let me in and we sat down in his living room. When he asked where I had been staying, I replied, "You really don't want to know." And he didn't; it was formality. My clothes could stay at his house, but not me.

As if he were trying to be honest, Fat Joe came back with "Okay, I don't. But I fucking do want to know if you can get me a laptop." Fat Joe explained that if I could get him an IBM 755 laptop, then he would pay me two thousand five hundred dollars, which would enable me to rent a room.

People often say one can sense weakness in a person by the worry-lines in the forehead or the contortions the skeletal frame makes through body posturing. Fat Joe smelled my body language as much as he sensed the desperation in the crack of my voice. I hated Fat Joe because he made me self-conscious about my homelessness. If I had begged him, perhaps I could have stayed at his house for a while, but he would have only used that as a way to feel superior, and I was trying to hold onto some pride. When I left Fat Joe's house wearing a dark suit with an ironed white shirt and burgundy tie, no one on the subway could guess I'd spent the last week in an abandoned car. As the old folks say, I clean up real good....

My movement mimics an invisible man's, the way I walk undetected and descend an escalator into a hole in the ground, through a turnstile, and into an opening subway car crowded with the perfume of rush hour. There are bodies close to mine, yet no one acknowledges that I exist. I'm hidden in the open. Broad daylight outside, and no one sees the who of what I am. Entering and exiting tunnels, moving from one state of being to the next—then stop, start over again, move into to the vast crowd of constricted faces passing in and out of my view. Doors opening and closing, and I exit at the FARRAGUT NORTH station—up the escalator, past the turnstile, and through another hole into a downtown with buildings.

The building is arbitrary among a row of structures that have nothing to do with each other, yet they are systematically aligned, cubed and squared as if linked together by human thought. Comprised of mortar and brick, the facial features of each building are an expression of a perceived freedom: beveled or cogent glass, sliding or revolving doors, independent company logos. Basically, they look the same.

The secretary thinks so, too. We all look the same: a suit, a tie, a clean-shaven face. A flesh machine working nine to five.

I walk past her in my vagueness, moving like the insignificance I have become, peering into cubicles and open doors until I find the laptop in a corner office overlooking K Street. Forty-five seconds, and cables become untangled and disengaged from the modem—the power shut off, the server no longer able to back up information, the screen dark. I scurry past the secretary filing her nails, take the back stairwell, skipping two cement steps at a time, and emerge into the lobby I just passed through. I breeze through the revolving door that instantaneously spits me back into daylight. I turn the corner and descend down another hole until I am no longer part of this landscape. The subway doors close. Still, I am invisible.

The tinted glass of the green van shielded the fact that all four
of us wore black turtlenecks. Black pants. Black jackets. Black ski
masks. An astrologist named Amali predicted our future on a cassette
tape. The voice kept reiterating that the stars had aligned at the
intersection of fate and destiny. For five minutes, we meditated to her
voice while the wind beat softly against the rolled-up windows. When
the tape finished, we exited the van. At two in the morning, the
weather had turned terrible, and white air streamed from our nostrils.
Thirty seconds, and Folks popped the lock on the glass door in front
of the men's clothing store. *Three minutes. We got three minutes.* I went
for dress slacks lined against the right wall, as Folks had instructed.
Connie darted to the back of the store and grabbed an armful of
designer suits. After retrieving the handcart from the back of the
van, Disco rolled it inside the store to the customer service desk. He
took a small crowbar from his back pocket and began to pry the safe
from its compartment underneath the cash register.

By the time Folks shouted *one minute*, I had made four
trips back and forth to the van. Folks took out a hammer wrapped
in a small dark towel and broke, in succession, all of the glass
encasements that housed the watches and jewelry.

The first time I had met Folks, he had a satchel full of
unset diamonds and a bag of authentic Rolexes. In the basement of
my house on Whittier Street, the old man of sixty-five had shown
me an infrared suit and told of how he entered buildings through
the rooftop, slid down on a rope, and cleaned a place out. He came
by my house one night, and the two-hour excursion that followed
took us up to a small town near Dover, where the steady snow was
coming down. Folks told me the best time to do dirt was in inclement
weather. He parked right in front of a clothing boutique next to
a jewelry store. Not even five minutes after he exited the car, he
motioned for me to come in through the front door of the boutique.
He then proceeded to cut a hole in the wall with a silent brick saw. I
became the lookout, and I swore the police were coming to lock us up
every time I saw headlights bouncing against the plate glass. Folks,
sensing my fear, said "police ain't coming," and, for some reason, I
believed him. I sat back and watched a real pro work with his tools
of the trade as he burrowed over to the other side and, within five
minutes, came out with a bag full of gold and diamonds.

But tonight, there were no infrared suits. This was a grab-all-you-can, fast as you can. No glass splashes, only thuds. Folks scooped the jewelry like he was on an assembly line. Disco loosened the safe until it popped free from the splintering wood, and leaned it back against the handcart. Everything slowed down. My legs felt like they were weightless in a pool of water, churning but hardly moving, but I kept going out of fear and adrenaline, endorphins electrifying my insides. When Folks yelled *time*, the store was a wreck and we were closing the doors to the van.

The flashing, one-eyed Cyclops whirled a glow of red and blue toward the flashpoint of the crime scene somewhere in Fairfax, the static transmission in the cop car blurting, *burglary in progress, burglary in progress.* On the opposite side of the median, a van with tinted windows zoomed north toward DC loaded with over five hundred suits, three hundred pairs of slacks, jewelry, and a safe.

Leaving the afterglow of Northern Virginia, we crossed the 14th Street Bridge into the District. The early morning night drew us farther uptown to a methodical right on K, then a left on 13th through a corridor of voluptuous butt and high-heeled stilettos selling fantasy presented as illusion. Traffic slowed almost to a stop. A quick surge around Logan Circle, and we crossed T Street. The rheumy gaze of derelict street men with whom I'd once carried the stick—meaning we ate in the same soup lines and kitchens, slept in the same shelters, cars, and abandoned buildings—swept casually over the van heading to Whittier and the house I now shared with Craig. I had almost certainly congregated with some of those men in the circle every morning, like a church flock with no Moses to guide us to an imaginary promised land, rudderless in a torrential downpour.

We hauled the safe and our new mountain of expensive clothes from the van through the basement door. Jacqueline and Craig rushed outside to help. Disco placed the safe on the handcart and, when he got in the house, broke out an assortment of power drills with special bits to penetrate the steel. Disco explained that he had to find the weak point close to the axis of the dial on the combination lock. Once he accomplished this, he studied the lock and manipulated the dial to align the lock's gates. Within minutes, the safe was opened, and seventeen grand was divided four ways. We each took about a hundred-plus suits, some slacks and jewelry. We sat up that night until there was no one left at the bar except Connie and me. I never understood her, but then too, I never tried. She was smart, having received an undergraduate degree in economics from

Howard. Maybe in some way I kept wondering how she pulled off what I could not, yet here we both were, partners, unable to escape street life. That night we made love at the bar while Jacqueline, her lover of two years, slept.

The next time I saw Folks, we were on our way to Nags Head, North Carolina. Folks had scoped the jewelry store months ago. He was good for that—riding with eyes open on the road, looking. Forty years of stealing had taught him to spot the easy score. In Nags Head, he discovered a way to get diamonds and a safe. Connie, Folks, and I drove down and checked into a hotel on Nags Head beach less than a quarter of a mile from the jewelry store that was located in a small plaza. Folks intended to drill a hole in the wall of the adjacent clothing store.

The first sign should have been Princess Diana's death that very morning. The second sign should have been the cop car passing by the plaza after midnight, which both Connie and I saw but Folks did not—at first. But when he did, just after pulling the yellow-handled screwdriver out of his pants pocket, *run*, he told us. *Run now.* We dashed back through the breezeway where we had been crouched moments before waiting for the door to open to smash, grab, and steal. Nothing but elbows and sneakers to the side entrance of the hotel, then up the stairs to the seventh floor where we were staying.

Folks discarded the screwdriver and walked back to the rental van. By the time the police pulled inside the parking lot to question him, we had gotten ghost. They searched Folks, found the hotel key, came to our room, and arrested us. We were placed in three police cruisers and questioned. When Connie panicked and tried to escape out the backseat through a rolled-down window, we were taken in on the spot.

Two months later, the three of us drove back to Nags Head for a show-cause hearing at the county courthouse. After the search for a national bail bondsmen by Craig in DC, after posting bail and driving back to DC to spend the next two months wondering what kind of case the prosecution had, and after reasoning that we would be released without show cause, we were in the courtroom, prepared to go back home.

That is, until the last officer took the stand to report that Ms. Connie Kingston of Washington, DC, had stated we had full intentions on breaking into the building. Folks and I looked at each other and lowered our heads. Up until then, all of the evidence had been hearsay, and we knew we were going to walk out of there free.

Instead, we walked out with our cases bound over to the grand jury and the possibility of jail time. The ride back was silent until we reached Portsmouth. Folks pulled off the main interstate.

Perhaps if I told you that it took sixty seconds for the gun to emerge from up under the car seat, you would call me a liar. So let me just say it was the biggest damn gun I had ever seen. Folks turned with the gun and pointed the barrel directly into Connie's face. He told her that if she wasn't the biological mother of their child, *he would blow her muthafuckin head off her shoulders.* As a matter fact, he still might *blow her fuckin head off.* Wrong place, wrong time. I'm trying to picture that—what it means to be headless, to be without a noggin, like, *what does that look like?* And what would become of the blood in the car—would we have to clean it?

You don't want to do this, is what I kept saying over and over. Perhaps I was trying to save my own hide more than that of the woman in the backseat. Murder is for a long time—longer than I wanted to find out. The judicial system handed out sentences like *from now on* to people involved in taking life, as well as those associated with taking that life—as in me. Connie sat like a deer, too scared to move because she was guilty of the unforgivable sin: she told. If Folks did not kill her, someone would. Nobody likes a snitch, and the word would travel long and fast as soon as we got back to DC. *You don't want to do this man,* I said for the fifth time, and he put down the gun, tucked it under the seat, and started the car engine. We drove back up the highway without sound. No radio, no cough, no *I gotta use the bathroom*—nothing.

When Connie moved out of the house, Craig and I became extra cautious in terms of our drug activities. Everybody we associated with had laid monetary bets on how long she would survive on the streets with the label of snitch. By this time Bobby, Craig's dad, was bringing close to three hundred pounds of cocaine a month to the DC area from Miami. Most of the kilos were already paid for, but because Craig was Bobby's son, he always looked out for him with five or ten kilos to sell on consignment. We mostly sold 62s, which is a sixteenth of a kilo, and 125s, which is an eighth of a kilo. The rest we cooked up into crack and had our people on the streets sell hand to hand. This access and my connections from my homeless days allowed me to flood 13th and T and 14th and V with drugs, as well as front packages to numerous dealers whom I once copped from. This gave me back the same power in the streets I had known in my Eleuthera days.

The low-level dealers, addicts, and street hookers called out to me—*Hook!*—as if I were a ghetto prodigal son, the one who made it out and could save them. And I ate it up, loved the idea of playing the ups game, which was: get up, dress up, and count up. Slowly, we began to put together a circle of friends who were all about hustling by hook or crook. Although he owned most of the product, I had just as much power and control as Craig because he trusted me more than anyone else. We had history together. Also, most of the people in the streets viewed me as one of their own who made it out the gutter. I looked out for the hookers and the street addicts on the regular by sliding them money or renting them a room for the month from time to time because I knew what that life was all about firsthand.

The one caveat that came with being in power was that we could never show weakness. If we ever did, someone would surely rob and murder us. Of this I was certain. So, my initial thought at 11:45 p.m. on a weekday in the back room of a row house facing the Old Soldiers' Home on 5th Street by the reservoir was, *this nigga gotta die tonight.*

I made the call to Foots from Bullet Head's place while opening a magnum of cognac. In the front room, there were drug dealers, con men, stickup kids and takeout artists salivating to revenge a wrong perpetrated on 5th and Whittier. Six hours earlier, Foots had waltzed into the four-bedroom house I shared with Craig, Craig's wife Donna, and my girl Beanie to buy an eighth of a kilo.

Craig and I had long been aware of Foots' dislike for us "down south" boys. For some unexplainable reason, he thought we were sexually involved with his wife, Chocolate, whom he'd married upon release from Lorton Prison. From our point of view, clearly he was tripping. Chocolate became the sister we never had, a woman who fit comfortably talking shit to men as much as she did to women. We were down like four flat tires as we braved multiple wind-swept nights under the vertiginous glow of the lampposts on T Street, churning out plastic baggies full of crack, seven days a week, three-sixty-five.

The phone rang. Chocolate picked up. I swirled the russet liquor around in a paper cup and asked for Foots. The background noise told me that Chocolate had an apartment full of streetwalkers who were tending to her every need in hopes of getting a chance to melt a white pebble in the corner of a metal crack stem. I've been over to her house when she had a girl washing dishes, one vacuuming, one doing her hair, and one bagging dope. She put those girls to work for that five-minute rush.

"Hook, I heard crazy-ass Punkin almost got you locked up last month. Bumshell told me Craig's old man was up from Miami with bricks. I hear you guys got it stacked, and that fool banging on the door. Mad cause you won't give her a hit. Scared she might miss something. Heard she woke the whole neighborhood. Threw a brick through your front door window. You know that bitch crazy!"

"Right," I said. Punkin had almost gotten us locked up. Three kilos in the house and her banging on the door, waking up the whole neighborhood. We had long parted ways since she had left me that fateful night in an abandoned car. But when I got back in the game, she'd found her way to Whittier one night and banged on the door until I opened it and gave her some coke.

I wondered if Chocolate knew what was going on.

"Let me speak to Foots. I need to ask him something."

The receiver went silent. Maybe she did know, but if she did, I couldn't tell. I swallowed the entire cup of liquor and let the taste crawl down my throat slowly, waiting for the burn to give me an edge.

"Yeah? What up, man. This me."

The funny thing about Foots was that we were tight at one time. I remember when he first came home from Lorton. To me, it was easy to tell when a dude was fresh out of the joint. The face was clear, pristine, the body cut up like a bag of dope from all the pull-ups and push-ups.

Foots' mistakes resided in his attempt to transform Chocolate into something she could never be: a housewife. It was like he never heard the saying *you can't turn a ho into a housewife*. No one could accuse Chocolate of being a street ho, but she was of the streets. Foots often called and talked about how he wanted Chocolate to stop doing hand-to-hand combat in the streets. I learned a long time ago to stay out of grown folk business, so I always just listened while he ran his mouth.

But something changed when he came home from that second stay in prison and started to hear how Craig and I had gotten tight with Chocolate while he was locked down. Then he started to understand the depth to which we were involved in this hustling game that he himself was trying to master. He found out that we weren't small-time hustlers trying to make three hundred dollars off an eight-ball. Someone had told him I had the Bahamas hook-up and Craig was running bricks from Miami. I think he got jealous, and our relationship deteriorated from that point on. Funny how people always think that 'cause you got the biggest sack, you trying to screw everything moving.

When he got on the phone, I could already feel his breathing patterns speed into a flurry of deep breaths preparing to justify his motive.

"Talk to me Foots, tell me what happened."

No sense beating around the bush. The lump in his throat cleared as I turned to watch Bullet Head oil his .44 in the other room. Curtis, the resident bodyguard, was breaking down his sawed off pump from where I sat, staring down both barrels, high off cocaine.

Disco, a natural born killer, was putting blow up his nose fast as he could funnel it through the hundred-dollar bill between his thumb and forefinger. He really had no stake in this drama except he loved to pull the trigger of a gun more than the he loved to stroke the torso of a woman. It had been six months since his wife had disappeared and was found in the trunk of a car in Charles County, and although the killer remained at large, everyone in the room knew who committed the crime.

"Man, you know how Donna be trying to talk to a dude like he ain't no man, and you know me slim, I ain't going for that."

True, I never liked Donna. Craig and I'd had a good set-up when she moved in. The kind of deals that went down, the cash fluttering through money machines, was astronomical. It was nothing to be counting anywhere from twenty to a hundred thousand on any given week. I never understood why Craig brought Donna home with him that night from the after-hours club on 9th and U. I mean, I'd known Donna since 13th and T, when we were all flesh and bones flapping in the wind. Those were the lean days when I really got introduced to DC and street life through Jo-Jo. Everybody on the block at that time did armed robberies, burglaries, sold dope or whatever to stay above water, and Donna walked the track like the rest of the hookers, selling her body to get high and earning a reputation for setting people up to get jacked.

Craig took her in and literally turned her into a "greater than" persona over night. She dripped diamonds and gold and counted the kind of money she had never laid eyes on before. This gave her the swag to try to talk to anybody any kind of way just because she was sexing Craig. We had words one night when she tried to regulate how much coke I had access to. That night I called Craig on the cell, and from that point on, she stayed out of my way. I knew who and what she was, but you can't tell another man about his woman.

Foots, on the other hand, had almost broken her jaw. And Craig was my homeboy, so that put me right in the middle of this shit.

"Yeah I know her mouth ain't right; but, man you can't do that," I said.

But Foots' fate had already been determined. He might as well have been on a ferry with Charon riding across the River Styx. The main purpose of this call was to find out what time he would be leaving the house. Maybe, in some way, I was giving him hope we could work this out, because he knew he fucked up royally when he violated the most sacred of creeds and hit another man's wife.

"Look, Foots. We need to rap about this."

Tangela, Disco's sister and Folks' young girlfriend, probably the prettiest woman I knew from this kind of life, came over and gave me a kiss on the cheek. The bulge of her Glock grazed my shoulder blade, then she whispered, "I'm going to personally put a hole in that muthafucka, baby."

"Man, I'm about to make a run, hit me up later." Foots hung the phone up.

This was the arrogance of Foots. Like what just went down was no big deal. Craig, who was huddled up talking with Bullet Head—a wise veteran of committing murderous acts, a legend inside and outside the penitentiary for his violent approach to personal matters—was diagramming the blueprint of how Foots would die tonight. The room was choked with marijuana smoke, cocaine dust, and hard liquor. Every person in the room was strapped with some type of metal device that killed, be it a gun or knife. Some of them would love nothing better than to push the edge of a steel blade through Foots' gut. This is how we acknowledged our love for each other.

I didn't want bloodshed, but this situation was like being sucked into a black hole from which there was no return. There were certain codes in the streets to live by. We were supposed to be big-time drug dealers, and this was the moment of truth. Foots, a man who had as many bodies behind him as Disco—or more—could not get away with hitting another man's wife. To not side with these men would mean I would be cast out of the pack. But more than that, to plead for Foots' life would jeopardize my own. We took two cars.

At 1:15 a.m., after about an hour wait, Foots trotted down the steps of his apartment building on 13th and Euclid. In one car sat Bullet and Craig. In the SUV, it was me, Curtis, Disco, and Tangela. Foots headed north toward Fairmont, then suddenly changed direction and darted across the street in the middle of traffic. He walked directly in our line of sight. Disco and Tangela were in the front seat whispering, *We got him. We got that clown. He ours.* We had the clearest shot as Foots came directly to the car parked in front of us, where someone sat waiting for him in the driver's seat.

I kept thinking to myself, *from this point on ain't no turning back. The streets adopt you fair and square. You are a thing now, not a person, not a human, but inhumane.* This wasn't what my mother had bargained for when I slid down her thighs prematurely and represented the possibility of all she had never achieved. I had spoken to my father two days earlier and told him a bunch of lies about how I was turning my life around. He knew I was lying, but he really did want to believe. And what would my little sister say? I had to make the choice between my family and "the pack." I thought about it all and said, *Fuck it—this nigga gotta die tonight.*

Foots got into the passenger's seat of the car. As soon as he slammed the door shut, Disco and Tangela exited the driver's and passenger's seats of our SUV. Curtis and I eased out of the back doors and positioned ourselves at the corner block of Clifton Street to make sure no one was coming. Curtis had his sawed-off under his coat, and I had a nine millimeter tucked in my waist. Disco and

Tangela walked up, holding their guns straight. They appeared at the right side of the car where Foots sat, and they fired, in rapid succession, eight gunshots into the windshield, the red-blue flame spitting from the pistols. The impressions of circular holes when the lead pierced the glass were swift and pronounced. Foots slumped down.

Nothing else to do—Foots dead.

The driver of the car sat stunned, but he was not the target, so he lived. He cranked up his car and sped away. At the same time, we hopped back in the SUV. Bullet pulled his car south and turned left on Euclid. We went north and turned right on Columbia.

All night we celebrated death. Patted each other on the back like good boys for a job well done. I didn't allow myself to think. I padlocked my feelings like I had taught myself to do years before when I first became homeless in DC. The streets and the people living within its boundaries beat me up so much that I eventually learned compassion was a sign of weakness.

In the morning, my friend Gary called.

"Man, you try to take Foots out last night?" I was still groggy from cognac and cocaine. I knew Gary could care less, so I'm wondering why he calling me with this bullshit.

"What the hell you talking 'bout?" I finally said through closed eyelids.

"Hook, ya'll gotta call this one. Dude, Foots is alive. None of those bullets hit him. He alive. It ain't his time, man. It ain't his time."

My eyes opened wide and I sat straight up.

If I had known what I know now, I would not have pulled into the next office complex. I would not have driven up the concrete ramp and parked on the second floor. But fate is an uncalculated science. My girlfriend Beanie and I would not have exited the light blue van and taken the back stairwell that lets out onto the second floor's carpeted hallway, nor would we have discussed the quick score for ten grand that we were about to make. But we did.

Within five minutes of picking the door lock, we knew our time had been wasted. Going in and out of each cubicle in the accounting firm quickly revealed cheap technology with no resale value. We didn't find the high-tech, state-of-the-art laptops we needed. So we retraced our steps back down the hall to the stairwell, down the stairs to the garage, and back to the van. When I opened the van's door, I glanced out the corner of my left eye and saw a flood of plainclothes police officers rushing toward us with guns in the air, yelling, *freeze!* Before *freeze* echoed off the garage walls, I was gone.

I ran, knowing I could not outrun the cold, abandoned buildings I'd once slept in amidst pain and urine-stained alleys. I could not return to the terrifying isolation of living at the edge of the world or going from homeless shelter to soup kitchen at the break of dawn in search of scrambled eggs and pancakes—so I ran harder, churned my elbows and knees faster.

The adrenaline thumping my chest provided the beat, the cadence to which my legs scissored. However, the police could run fast, too, their thick-soled shoes pressing against the ground, an authoritative voice commanding, *Stop or I'll shoot!* How could these men and women in diligent pursuit know that death didn't mean anything when I had lived in death's presence, courted its beautiful ugly, and the fear of dying proved to be no greater than the fear of living? Then again, it's funny how, from two stories up, falling downward with a body weight of a hundred ninety-five pounds, is not even two seconds to the bottom. That is what I discovered when I leaped from the second floor of the garage. Wind would not make sails of my body mass and float it over Interstate 240, so I dropped fifty feet straight down onto the grassy knoll—I dropped like I was on a mission, trying to angle my body, to will it against the incline. I thought I might die.

The plainclothes police officer dropped, too, and at that

moment, when I glanced back, our eyes locked. I understood we were both committed, dedicated to an end result. I hit the incline, tucked and rolled, and so did the plainclothes police officer.

Before the highway, there rested a thicket of shrubbery and trees, a small forest in the city. I thought I could break through it. I thought I would be free until a cluster of vines and sticker bushes latched onto my sweatshirt and jeans, twisting and contorting my body. I was a dangling fly caught in a web. The plainclothes officer who had dropped with me appeared first, his weapon drawn, ordering me to *freeze*. I remained suspended as part of the vine cluster. Two other officers appeared next, handcuffed me, and then untangled my body from the stickers and vines. All three of us walked back down the path to their waiting police car.

Riding in the backseat, handcuffed, I watched a man and a woman with interlocking fingers take in the night air on the main boulevard. It would be almost five years before my laughter would mimic that of the teenagers in the car stopped at the traffic light to my left. I was going to prison, and not one single person on the street tonight would miss me. There would be no love letters or visits. *Daddy*, I wanted to call. *Daddy*. I wanted to chase clusters of fireflies, pull honeysuckle stems and smell the South's ambrosia. I wanted my mom to yell at the top of her lungs: *Boy, brang your hardheaded ass here*. I wanted the love I had spit into my parents' faces to come back and baptize me.

I wish I could say that the process from booking to the jail cell is a blur, but it is not. Nothing happens so quickly that one cannot remember. The events are chronological. The police drop you off handcuffed at the station. They collect information: name, address, priors, and next of kin. You are placed in a holding cell that refuses to let you think outside the context of confinement. You are in conversation with the concrete walls, asking, *Why, dumbass mutherfucker—why*, even though the answer has been gradually coalescing, nurturing itself throughout the years you have been throwing your life away. This is not a test where you will be returned to your regularly scheduled programming. There is never complete silence in the holding cell. Too many packed bodies for isolation.

My fingerprints and mugshot are taken. I shower with the guards watching me. Next, I am sprayed with insecticide to make sure I don't have lice or crabs. Then, I am placed into general population to wait four weeks for the appointment of a lawyer who will, upon our first meeting, ask me to plead guilty, because I am.

Guilt is always a formality with public defenders. The only thing I can do is try to limit the number of years I will be away from society. The public defender will tell me this. I think of my limited possibilities that third night I lie on my bunk until I become an apparition and float outside the frame and skin clinging to my soul. In this out-of-body experience, all I can do is examine my state of wretchedness—my past, present, and future—while balled in the fetal position. That night, I would close and open my eyes to razor and brick and come to understand that I had to free my mind of the way I narrated my life, or I would forever be caught within concrete and iron.

Randall. We are more alike than different. If you only knew. She was the heaviest piece of power I ever wrapped my hands around. The sexy wooden handle and her long nose gave Ms. .357 character. She was my first, and I was scared to hold her. She was forced on me. It was warm that October afternoon. I remember exactly what I had on: blue tank top, gray sweat pants, and a pair of white, sky-and-navy-blue sneakers. I didn't plan on staying outside on the block long, but I was waiting for Dred to bring me some chocolate to smoke. Instead of standing around, I decided to take a walk to Marcy Place.

When I got to the corner of Walton and Marcy, this Puerto Rican kid named Feecha approached me and told me that Sin was looking for me. Feecha was cool, but I'd never trusted him. He was a shiesty individual, a small-time hustler who would do anything for a dollar, even if that meant stealing from his best friend. I always treated him with a long-handled spoon. When he told me Sin was looking for me, I was surprised.

Sin and I had bad history together. A tall, slender Moreno with skin that went from caramel to sun-drenched bronze, his eyes were hazel-green, constantly changing color depending on his clothes and his mood. There were permanent circles that shadowed his features; he had the kind of darkness under his eyes that even make-up could not erase. He kept his brown hair faded low with a crown of light brown specks along the root of his hairline. When I first met Sin, I was attracted to him; he was incredibly handsome and charming. His manner was intriguing, though his insecurities outweighed the good of his character. He was controlling, and I was a free spirit exploring life. I refused to take him seriously because I wanted to live without restrictions. At the time, I was in love with another man. I broke Sin's heart when I told him the truth.

I remember that day clearly. Sin was upset because I had promised to take him to dinner the night before and left him waiting. I made him feel like a fool. He knew better than to knock on my door looking for me because of the way my parents felt about black people. Instead, Sin waited until the next morning to approach me while I was on my way to work. I saw him standing at the corner of 170th Street by the Chinese restaurant. I walked across the street as if everything was normal and tried to give him a kiss. He greeted my lips with the receiver of a public phone, then grabbed me by the hair and beat my head with the handle. I was screaming, but no one did anything. He dragged me by the hair down the block to Townsend Avenue toward 171st and continued hitting me. When he kicked me in the stomach, I threw up blood, and he stopped for a little while, but then kept on. He was persistent in questioning me about who I was with. I was adamant about not revealing that I was in love with another man because it would only add to the damage to my face.

I remember screaming at the people passing by, begging them for help, but no one seemed to care. There was an unspoken fear of this man—or animal—and I couldn't understand how people pretended as if they couldn't hear me, as if they weren't seeing him hit me. I cried and wondered why they didn't care enough to intervene or at least call the police. The fight was out in the open, across the street from a public elementary school.

After what seemed like hours of abuse, I told Sin the truth. I knew it would only make matters worse, but at that moment I was in so much pain, and I wanted to hurt him any way I could. Once I confessed, he went crazy on me, and if it wasn't for Kingston, I don't know what would've happened. Kingston was a skinny Jamaican with locks that hung down to his waist. The hair on his face was burly and untamed, which made him appear rough, although he wasn't. He knew me from Taylor Place, where he hustled smoke for the Jamaican Brothers, three guys who ran the marijuana distribution in my area. I was best friends with the youngest one, Biggs. Being that Kingston knew that me and Biggs were tight, he defended me. Kingston stood up to Sin and said, "Wha' de bloodclot go on round here, why da fuck ya beaten on she, ya crazy, look at she face, why don't ya hit a real man, ya fuckin' pussyclot, ya know she can't defend she, ya ain't no real gangsta, come off she, and ya best not try nothin' else to she, ya hear me?"

As soon as Kingston reached over to grab my arm, Sin pushed his hand away and screamed, "Mind ya business son, this ain't got shit to do with you. That's my shorty, and she disrespected me."

I remained standing there before them with my head bowed, nose and mouth leaking red pain, crying, shaking my head, whispering, "That's bullshit, I ain't his girl."

As I wiped my face with my sleeve, I slightly lifted my head, and Kingston looked at me.

Without saying a word, he quickly grabbed my arm and started walking toward his girlfriend Hope's building. Sin tried to come between us, but Kingston warned him to leave us alone before the situation became personal.

I know many people saw what happened on Townsend Avenue and didn't move to help me. It made me contemplate the many other things that people see but do not witness. It's still difficult to comprehend how the average person refused to help me; it was a bottom-of-the-gutter muthafucka who played the good Samaritan. Who would've thought Sin would respect a man smaller than him?

When we got to Hope's house, I immediately went to the bathroom and started to clean up. I sat down on the toilet while Hope dressed my cuts and bruises with A&D ointment and bacitracin. We didn't talk about what happened. She let me be quiet, trapped in my own thoughts, while she attempted to mend the wears and tears on my skin.

When I got up to look in the mirror, I did not recognize myself. My eyes were practically swollen shut. My lips were torn and inflamed. My nose appeared distorted because it was larger by the bridge. There were several knots and bruises by my chin, cheekbones, and forehead. I had pieces of glass stuck in my face and hands. What I remember most was Sin lifting my neck and punching my throat.

When they walked me home, all I could think about was my mother and how I was going to explain my appearance. I never told my family it was Sin; instead, I told them I got jumped. I kept that incident to myself because I didn't want to get my family involved. My mother would have called the police, and I didn't want that reputation. I was afraid Sin would try to hurt my parents because of the finger pointing.

Sin tried to reconcile with me, but I always dismissed his efforts. Like the time he sent me a painting, delivered by a little kid from my building. When the kid told me to look out the window to see who sent it, I quickly snatched the painting and ran to the window before my mother could question the gift. Out went the painting, and I saw Sin watching from across the street, his eyes stuck on the painting swooping down four flights. Before the piece hit the pavement, he yelled, *Bitch, I hate you,* and all I heard was the crash that followed.

About two years passed before I saw Sin in the neighborhood again. He had opened a crack spot on Marcy. We didn't speak to each other; instead we stared into each other's eyes until we were both out of eyeshot. I guess he didn't know what to expect from me, and I didn't know if he still held a grudge against me for not taking him seriously. Whenever we did see each another, I would usually be in a car, and he would be standing on the corner of Marcy. A sense of fear and anxiety always came over me whenever our eyes met. I observed his routine and made an effort to stay out of the neighborhood as much as I could. I tried to shun him because I didn't want to stir up any repressed feelings. Avoiding him was hard because he was getting money on the block but I kept myself surrounded by people. That way if he tried to approach me, I wouldn't be alone. He never tried to talk to me when other people were around because he didn't want to make it seem like he still had feelings for me.

That is why when Feecha told me that Sin was looking for me, it caught me by surprise. Feecha mentioned he was in the stash house, but I had no idea where the stash house was. I didn't want to seem interested in Sin, so I ignored Feecha and sent him to the store to get a Dutch. He rode down the block on his bike to the bodega. When he came back with the cigar, he told me Sin was waiting for me across the street from 15 Marcy Place. I took the cigar and walked down the block to meet him, knowing whatever he wanted to tell me would not be good. A part of me wanted to run home, but a greater part of me wanted to face him and my fears. Walking down the block, I began to think about all the things Sin put me through when we had interacted with each other. The naïve part of me wanted to believe his intentions were to apologize, but logic overrode that notion. My heart felt as if he owed me something more than peace of mind when I walked through my neighborhood.

When I approached him, instead of talking, I lit a cigarette and waited for him to speak. He stared at me for a while before he said anything. He studied my face as if he could read my thoughts. When he finally spoke, his opening was cold with no apology attached. "What's good, L? I know you on a paper chase, and I need someone I can trust to hold my car down for me. Can you drive my car to an indoor parking lot and hold my keys down until I call you? I'll pay you a G." He did not expect me to be as calm as I appeared.

Sin didn't mention anything else, but I imagined there would be either drugs or weapons in the car. Instead of asking about the details of the act, I told him I would think about it over a smoke. He began to walk into the building, and I followed. Trailing behind him, I began to question myself: *how could I be manipulated into this situation for a measly thousand dollars?* At the time, it seemed like easy cash, and Sin knew he could use money to lure me back into his life. There was something about the suaveness in his tone that made me leery of the situation. How could he trust me if I was the same person that broke his heart? Maybe he felt he could trust me because I never told on him.

My addiction blinded me, and I pacified the situation in an effort to get high. I thought I could smoke a blunt with him and resolve our differences before agreeing to his proposition. I followed him up the stairs and into an apartment. He had the keys to all the locks. Naturally, I assumed the apartment was his, until I saw a lady come out of one of the bedrooms. After observing her erratic behavior, it was obvious she was a drug addict. The apartment was immaculate, and I analyzed the surroundings, trying to define the status of this woman. I didn't know if she was a dope fiend or a crackhead. Dope fiends are obsessively clean, and judging from the appearance of the apartment, I could say she was a heroin addict, but the constant tweaking ultimately labeled her a crackhead. I felt sorry for her; we locked eyes for a moment until Sin threw her a rock. He paid her in crack pieces, as most dealers pay off fiends who house their supply. Once she got the rock, she locked herself back in the bedroom, her addiction keeping her confined and Sin fully in control.

His possessiveness of the space did not surprise me. He offered me something to drink, and I told him I would grab it, because I didn't trust him. I went to the kitchen and rinsed out a drinking glass. I looked on top of the sink for a dishrag so I could use soap to wash it. I heard a knock at the door. I suspected it was one of the fellas from the block coming to re-up. Sin walked up to the door, looked through the peephole, and opened it. In entered two Spanish guys. I could hear them, but I could not see their faces. At that moment, a part of me wanted to leave. I didn't know these men and I didn't want to be involved this deep. I was around the corner from my house, and if anything went down, it would be difficult to escape retaliation because this was my hood; where else could I go?

They walked into the apartment and entered the living room. I found the rag and lathered it up, slowly washing the cup, completely ignoring them. A tall, skinny *blanquito* walked in, while the other—a stocky *trigueño*—trailed behind. The *trigueño* had a telephone box in his hand. I couldn't help noticing it because it was the only thing either one carried. The guys were clean-cut and did not appear to be customers. I knew somebody was buying or selling something, but it wasn't for personal use. After I rinsed all the soap off of the cup, I looked into the refrigerator, pulled out a container of orange juice and poured it into the glass.

I stood there in the kitchen for a while, drinking, wanting to walk out. I worried about them seeing me, whether I left or stayed in the apartment. When I finally walked over to the table in the living room, both guys watched me as I grabbed the lighter off the table. I searched for the Newports in my pocket and pulled one out. Both men then asked if they could have one. I kept my cool and handed each a Newport. I turned and sat on the sofa and lit my bone in silence. Sin told me to roll up and threw a bag of chocolate at me. I told him I needed another Dutch, but before he got a chance to ask, the light-skin guy offered to go to the store.

I walked him toward the door and handed him a dollar while Sin stayed back. When we were making our way toward the exit, he introduced himself as Blanco and asked me for a light. I stared silently into his light brown eyes and gave him fire. After locking the door behind him, I walked back into the living room and sat at the table crushing the chocolate, pulling out seeds and stems, cleaning the bud before I twisted up. Sin and the other guy began to weigh the contents in the phone box. Sin had a small scale, which appeared to be more of an inconvenience than an asset. They had to divide the coke into four sections in order to weigh it. When they finally finished, the content was placed back into the box. I waited to see if money was going to be exchanged, but Sin did not pull out a dime.

Sin sat on the sofa looking pensive, with his shirt covering two guns hidden between the sofa cushions. I noticed one of the pistols sticking out and gave him a look. He checked himself and covered the handle. The guy began to feel uneasy, sensing tension in the air. He began to tell Sin that he wished he had done the deal in Washington Heights. "Easy, Montana," was all I heard Sin say, over and over again. Sin was a snake. He got the dude to trust him by lending them his car to pick up the work. The car wasn't worth shit, but these cats were fooled by the gesture. Montana kept looking out the window for Blanco, hoping his friend would return quickly. I could see Sin and Montana clearly from the top end of the table. Montana stood erect by the window in front of me and Sin sat patiently to the right of me, on the couch, in between the two pistols covered by the XXL blue-and-white-striped T-shirt.

While Montana was looking out the window trying to rush Blanco to come back to the apartment, Sin shouted, "Tell him to get me a Yoo-hoo." When Montana turned around to face the two of us, what awaited him was an unexpected introduction to Ms. .357 and

Mr. 9mm. Poor Montana stood stunned and peed himself in disbelief. Everything was quiet for a brief moment, as if the world stopped moving. Then silence broke with a knock. Montana yelled, *¿Que lo que esta pasando?* What the fuck is this? The knock at the door turned into bangs, followed by kicks that echoed through the living room where the three of us stood—two in a panic and one in control.

I looked at Sin, "Why the fuck you gettin' me involved in this bullshit, this is between ya, I ain't makin' money off this shit."

"Shut the fuck up, L. Do what I say. Tie this nigga up and lay him on the floor. The tape is by the radiator behind you."

"I don't wanna—"

"I don't want to hear that shit, bitch! Empty out his pockets. Take off his chains. Don't hesitate. Get the tape—it's behind you. Just do it, quick."

I asked Montana to relax so we both wouldn't get hurt, and I told him to cross his arms on his chest and taped his entire upper body until the tape was gone. I had no idea what I was doing, and then I laid him face down on the hardwood floor and sat on top of his butt.

I didn't know what to do next, when Sin put her in my hands. "Hold this down while I search him." Sin reached into Montana's pocket and pulled out a satin black pouch and threw it on the floor by my feet. He reached for the other back pocket, pulled out a wallet and retrieved five hundred dollars. He took a good look at the address and placed the ID card back into his pocket. Sin snickered, "You ain't got no jewels, Papi?" But Montana was speechless. Blanco continued to pound on the metal door with his fists, as if the noise could stop what was already in progress. Sin told me to aim the gun at Montana while he brought Blanco back into the house. He walked toward the door and left Ms. .357 with me for protection. I held her, amazed at the weight of the instrument. I was trying to maintain control when I heard Sin struggling with Blanco at the door. I couldn't see what was happening because I was on the floor.

And that's when Montana chose to break free. The motherfucker broke loose from the duct tape. I tried to put pressure on his back with the gun so he couldn't move, but he was fighting me off. He tried to turn around and grab the gun. I began to scream, "He got loose, he got loose," and in an effort to protect me, Sin came runnin.'

Everything got blurry for a second. A shot rang out, and it echoed in my ear. I checked Montana's breathing. "He's still breathing, he's still breathing." Sin leaned over Montana, said, "You aight, son?"

I was in shock, mumbling to myself, "This fuckin *pendejo* asking this *cabron* if he okay and he fuckin almost shot my ass? Wannabe hero-ass nigga, you ain't trying to fight me now with a bullet in ya, *maricón*." Montana's still body weighed heavy over Ms. .357, his hands too weak to wrap around her handle. I struggled to lift his dead weight up and grabbed her right from under him.

I heard a shout at the door, "L, get the box, and get out." I grabbed the telephone box with the work, held Ms. .357, and ran out the door. Blanco tried to grab my arm and asked me what happened, but I shook him off and told him, "Check ya man." When I reached the exit of the building, Sin was waiting. "Gimme the box and the gun, here the keys, the car is down the block on Jerome."

I ran toward the car, and when I looked up while I was opening the car door, I saw Blanco coming for me with a Rambo knife in hand. For some reason I couldn't get the car to start. I felt him getting closer, then suddenly the engine of the Buick LeSabre came to life and I fled the scene, eating the next two red lights in the process. I drove up Mount Eden Avenue across the Concourse toward the park near Lebanon Hospital. I needed to smoke a blunt and relax, but I didn't know where to go. I decided to go to Tati's because she lived in a private house, and I could park the car in the garage. Tati lived on the other side of town. I jumped on the highway by the Jerome Avenue entrance, and took the Cross Bronx Expressway. When I got to her house, she was cooking buttered salmon and potatoes. I rolled up a blunt and began telling her what happened. "Girl, let me tell you what this nigga Sin did...."

I was waiting for that 187 to pop up on the screen of my pager for two days before he called. On my birthday, October 12, 1999, Sin called my house from central booking.

"Hello, L."

"Yeah, who's this?"

"It's me, Sin. I got fuckin' locked up 'cause of this shit."

"When?"

"I went to Able's house after the club. The police came a few hours later looking for me. They putting my paper work through the system and I'm waiting to see the judge. Can't you leave for a few months?"

"No, where the fuck I'mma go? I still have that fed case open, and I'm out on bond. I hope you didn't mention my name in any way."

"Nah, nah, but I just don't want conflicting stories."

"What did you tell them? What the fuck you mean, conflicting stories? What did you say?"

"I didn't say shit, you selfish bitch. You out in the street and I'm in jail and all you can think about is your PC. What? You a bullshit gee? You need to give my girl Samantha the car so they can take that work out of town and flip the material."

"What the fuck all that has to do with me? I just want my cut, and I don't give a fuck what you do with the work."

"How much you want?"

"Half."

"You a selfish bitch. I haven't even got paid off the work and you already saying you want half. I have to break Able off for moving the material."

"I don't give a fuck about Able and your business with him, that's not my concern. I just want to get paid for my services."

"Fuck you, bitch. It was my blicky; you ain't set it up—I did. We shouldn't even be discussing this over the jack. Just give my girl the car."

"Tell that bitch to bring my money when she comes or all that shit in the car will disappear."

"Yo, I got mad clothes in there and so do she, don't be selling my shit."

"I won't sell the stuff if you pay me my money."

"You greedy bitch. I'm gonna have my bitches see you."

The line got cut off. I didn't hear from him for another couple of days. His girlfriend arrived at my door unannounced, but I knew Samantha from my neighborhood, and we'd never had problems. I talked to her and asked about my money. She let me know that she didn't have any money to give me, but that she would try to find a way to pay me. I told her I couldn't give her the car unless I got paid.

Samantha left my house upset. The following week she returned. By that time the car was crashed and all the clothes were gone. I had lent the car to my boyfriend Toño and his friend, who was sleepin' with Tati at the time. Those niggas crashed the car and brought it back to me like that. I wasn't even there when it happened. I couldn't tell Samantha or Sin that Toño and his boy did it because I was afraid he would send guys after them. That night they brought me back the car fucked up, I knew for sure I wasn't gonna get no money from Sin, so I went and sold some of their clothes and jackets to his boys and other people from the hood. When Samantha came to see me about the car and clothes, I let her know the details, but the truth is, I was nervous as hell.

She understood that the car was crashed before we walked toward the garage and that she'd need a tow truck to get it out. I mentioned how we could go head up in the hallway if that's what she wanted, so it looked like she was representing for her man, but she wasn't on it like that. She just wanted to get whatever articles of clothing were left. I realize then that she was living in the street with him. I knew Sin was going to be upset with me, but I felt played. I was scared to walk around my neighborhood because of Montana. I didn't know if they were following me.

Sin being in jail was none of my business. He never should have gone to Able's house knowing Blanco knew the address. Those guys didn't know who I was. I stayed at Tati's house for the remainder of October. By mid-November, the cops were beginning to knock on my mother's door. The first time, I didn't answer. The second time they came, they knocked both at the door and on my fire escape window, as if I were already guilty. I opened the door and the police lied and said they had a warrant for my arrest. I asked to see the warrant, and they told me to shut the fuck up and placed my hands behind my back. This lady detective who looked like a football player, with jersey and all, was my arresting officer. She turned me over and lifted my shirt to see my right shoulder. When she noticed my tattoo, she said I needed to go down to the precinct for a lineup. I was confused. Initially she had said I was under arrest, and then she mentioned a lineup. I didn't know what was happening, and my poor mother was a mess. She couldn't understand why they were taking me with them, and she asked to come with me, but they would not allow her to ride in the vehicle. She immediately walked to the 44th Precinct, which is about a block or two away from where we live, and waited for my arrival. After I was selected from the lineup, the officers told her to go to Bronx Criminal Courthouse so we could communicate. They were not going to release me.

I stood in the day room with an orange jumper tied at the waist, the sock slit between my big toe and second one lodged into a pair of county-issued flip flops. I listened to Pat Parker, a social worker employed by the Department of Health and Human Services, tell me and a group of twenty inmates how words would be our healing power. She wanted us to get in touch with the traumatic experiences that had brought us to "the bricks."

The Department of Health and Human Services designed Jail Addiction Services (JAS) in the Montgomery County Detention Center as a place to take inmates away from the day-to-day brutality of prison life, where a homemade shank always lurked inside someone's hand. In JAS, inmates could share their life experiences and hopefully find threads of commonality through which to address behaviors of aggression and deviancy. The main reason I applied to participate in the program was because I could get time reduced from my sentence. I had been charged with three counts of theft by possession and one count of second degree burglary—each count carrying a maximum sentence of twenty years. I was facing a total of eighty years. On my second legal visit, my lawyer told me that if I went to trial and lost, I would get the maximum for wasting the court's time. In preliminary talks, the prosecutor had mentioned the possibility of a five-year cap if I pleaded guilty. That meant the most I could receive was five years. I went into JAS hoping to reduce that number.

Every Thursday, Pat led a discussion around the dynamics of group interaction and how we inmates could benefit from written dialogue. The first assignment she gave was a series of questions that made us look introspectively at our behavior. She methodically explained that, in order to get to the root of pain and trauma, there had to be some kind of outward expression that originated internally, and that placing words on the page could free one of pain and guilt.

Maybe she was talking to me when she said these words. Writing was something I'd never considered growing up. I had not talked to my family in six months, and they did not know I was incarcerated. I would be sentenced soon and knew I needed to call and make amends to those who loved me the most.

That night, by the afterglow of a quarter moon outside my cell window, I stared at two simple questions on the sheet of paper Pat had given me. The first one was: DO YOU FEEL THAT AN

139

I wrote:

> My parents have been greatly disappointed by my life choices and my inability to grasp the concept of life and its responsibilities. During our sometimes-tumultuous, sometimes-joyous relationship, our ties have been severed because of my inexcusable and self-destructive nature. My actions over the years have slowly opened a deep wound, inflicting tremendous pain; only, every time, my parents' unyielding love outweighs the lacerations I've created. Their love for me outstretches bitterness and hatred. However, it is difficult for me, after all the forgiveness and openheartedness they have shown me, to have a relationship without feeling guilt. They did not, and do not, deserve to endure so much humiliation because of me.

The words came effortlessly and honestly, and for the first time in a long time, I cried. My tears fell softly onto the yellow legal pad as I transcribed my guilt. The second question was just as tough as the first: DO YOU FEEL WORTHLESS AS IT RELATES TO YOUR CURRENT SITUATION? For the first time in a long time, I was being forced to examine myself from the inside out.

> As I meditate and search within myself to locate the reasons why I am incarcerated, I know that I have not been all that I could have been up to this point in my life. I have shortchanged and deprived myself of the quality of life that comes with accepted social behavior. However, to call myself worthless would be to start putting nails in my coffin. I am not resolved to giving up and accepting that my life will only consist of drugs, hustling, repeated failure, prison, and eventually death. My mind cannot conceive of such a notion. Call it vanity, arrogance, or whatever you must. I categorize it as the will and the desire to change, to want a better way of life—one that I know is obtainable.

At the following group session I read the answers to those questions just as I'd written them on paper. I was finally gut-wrenchingly honest with myself, and I actually believed the words coming out of my mouth.

For the first time in my life, I wanted to write. I began to read more books from the prison library, starting with *The Autobiography of Malcolm X: As Told to Alex Haley*, Nathan McCall's *Makes Me Wanna Holler*, and Carl Upchurch's *Convicted in the Womb*. These authors spoke to me as if they understood. For instance, in *The Autobiography of Malcolm X*, I identified with Malcolm's street persona before prison. I had snorted cocaine, been a two-bit hustler and part-time pimp; I felt like we were kindred spirits. As Malcolm rises in the text from prison to become one of the most respected men in American history, I rose with him in the confinement of my cell. The famous picture of Malcolm looking out the window with a M1 carbine in his right hand—barrel turned up and trigger finger cocked at the ready—became a recurring image in my head.

I fell in love with language and likened Malcolm's transformation to the one occurring within me at Montgomery County Detention Center. I had swift-talked people out of their money and distributed drugs within the community I claimed I loved; perhaps a jail cell would be the only way to prevent the impending train wreck.

Malcolm, along with Upchurch and McCall, inspired me to want to be a writer. Their books became guides on how to properly use punctuation, grammar, and syntax—skills I had failed to master in college because I did not take reading and writing seriously; I was too occupied with being introduced to cocaine and drug smuggling. I read so much that when I fell asleep and dreamed, I re-enacted the stories and scenarios read earlier in the day: I was McCall running across the yard to join in the fight with Pearly Blue and Joe Ham, but I hesitated because I understood I needed to distance myself from the past and make good decisions. I was Upchurch undergoing "deniggerization," taking college courses in prison, discovering William Shakespeare, James Baldwin, Fyodor Dostoevsky, and Mark Twain. Their voices showed me the proper placement of verbs and nouns to create cohesive sentences that untangled my own voice and gave me speech.

The reality of Roxbury Correctional, as with any prison, is rooted in the idea that you cannot leave by your own free will—the key word being free. Walking from intake into and across the prison yard, taking in the pristine lawns and clean sidewalks, you get a sense of false security. You could be visiting a gated liberal arts college campus in a rural town if not for the razor wire circling the complex. But the Rottweilers' snapping jaws immediately destroy this fantasy.

A few paces farther, and the guard tower comes into focus against the backdrop of a cobalt sky. You can't help but think about the index finger willing to squeeze the trigger—the scope, barrel, and mirrored shades following every inmate's footstep.

The first night: 11:00 p.m. lock-in instigated a crippling silence in Cell 16 until the doors rolled back at 4:30 for breakfast the first morning. Our cells emptied into a stream of human flesh migrating toward the dining hall, which was a hundred yards opposite the housing unit. Our bodies blended together effortlessly. We could have been a herd of cattle going to graze. Midway to the entrance, with the sun's orange peeking through dawn's steel gray, a man moaned and dropped to the ground with a shank protruding from his stomach. Breakfast had to be eaten, so we each stepped over the bloody body.

I was told it would take about two years before the judge would hear my motion for reconsideration. After I received the maximum five-year cap on four felony counts, my court-appointed lawyer submitted the request before I was transported upstate, but cautioned against hope for an early release. A modification of sentence was left solely to the judge who tried the case. The judge had the power to revisit a sentence and reconsider the time given if the prisoner could show just cause. There was no guarantee the motion would be granted, and if it was, chances were slim, even next to none, that a judge would modify my sentence.

Before I left for upstate, Pat Parker called me into her office in the county jail and asked me not to stop writing. She thought I had talent. No one had ever told me this. But more than that, Bunnie Boswell, who ran the JAS, said if I agreed to participate in a two-year drug program in Durham, she might be able to persuade the judge to commute my sentence and have me placed there.

In the meantime, I tried to remember every bit of advice given to me in county jail from the old heads, the ones in and out of prison so frequently they acquired invaluable knowledge. Definite no-nos were: Don't borrow nothing from nobody. Don't jump the line—any line. Be respectful of the phone and a man's religion. Don't get caught in a lie. You steal and get caught, you could lose your life. Always keep your sneakers on because you may have to fight at any given moment. Don't fight fair. Don't get punked, or you may be somebody's punk. Always keep a shank close by, and don't be afraid to use it; if you are, again, you may lose your life.

Roxbury Correctional Institution is located in Hagerstown, Maryland. It's flanked by stoic mountains rising from the east and west. Dairy farms add a certain presence as the wind whistles through the valley. The heaviest concentrations of men there hail from Baltimore, which helps create the Washington/Baltimore divide. Both are fairly large cities with high crime and drug rates. They are thirty minutes apart by car, and within both inner cities there is an unwritten rule of competition. The unwritten rule in Roxbury dictated that I associate myself with Washington folk or risk being eaten alive by Baltimore.

There were folks already in my housing unit who could vouch for my street cred, that I was a dude who played as fair as one could in the cutthroat hustling game. This was a place where a reputation on the outside could help your status on the inside. My first cellmate, Deboe, was from the District. Before we could get to any type of meaningful conversation, we performed the ritual of male bonding to see if each of us really knew the streets of DC like we claimed. I could tell Deboe was suspicious of me, but by the same token, I was suspicious of him. After small talk, the conversation turned to how dudes sold fake televisions in the box to unsuspecting victims over on Minnesota Avenue. Deboe mentioned the Black Hole and Celebrity Hall hosting all the live go-go parties back in the day, and I concurred. We both reminisced about the heyday of Portland Avenue and the Jamaican wars during the late '80s. This barrage of questions and answers continued until I was deemed legitimate.

Six years into a sixty-year sentence for a murder that occurred in Prince George's County, Deboe rambled in a raspy voice about why he hated Baltimore dudes. "Them jokers funny, homie. Can't trust 'em 'cause most of 'em dope fiends for that heroin. Don't expect them to have your back. Naw, don't do that. If anything, they gon' light your ass up."

Deboe was twenty-two years old, and the state of Maryland had tried and sentenced him as an adult. He knew nothing about manhood but what he learned behind iron bars. The older inmates served as his role models and mentors—the closest thing to a father he would ever know. Roxbury is where he grew up and perhaps would die.

The next day, I moved across the hall, in with Big Cheese in Cell 17, and Kevin moved out of Cell 17 and into 16 with Deboe. Kevin and Deboe were around the same age and had a thriving illegal commissary hustle with a hundred percent interest rate. They wanted to consolidate their operation and expand.

Big Cheese was here on drug possession charges and had two years to go before his release date. At the age of thirty-two, he claimed he was tired and that the best way to get out of here early and alive was to hang with dudes who had something to lose. He told me that cats close to parole—considered short-timers, meaning five years or less—tended to stay out of trouble and not get involved in fights. For the next year, we would come to know each other's struggles. We would see things happen that we will never speak about.

Night. A deafening silence filling every inch of the housing unit. Every stir amplified by the isolation of a closed cell door. The beat-thump began simple enough: that intense percussive called go-go, drawing on West African influences, the indigenous music of the District of Columbia. Two doors down in Cell 19, Josephus got go-go fever induced by mail call after shift change. Five years into an eight-year bid, his girlfriend, who stayed in Clifton Terrace, informed him she would no longer vigil the memory of his street heroics. His image had faded from DC's landscape, and so would she.

There was no question the right fist was balled, driving the cadence like a conductor calling out to a crew of gandy dancers laying eight-foot railroad track: *Get a grip in ya hand, whoa na, work wit it chillin', whoa na.* The left hand, palm open, balanced the driving narrative of gut-bucketed pain, much like a mauling does six-inch spikes into the crossties: *Let it swang on down, whoa na.*

A combination of spirituals, blues, work songs, and field holler Josephus banged, pulling each man to the edge of his bunk to listen to the coded message thumped on a metal desk doubling as a djembe. For five minutes, he held us hostage with the same beat—the same goddamn beat, exhibiting how written language can kill the human spirit. Then he released us to a much faster, more complicated syncopation, the reverberated echo unique to each man's current temperament, so we each wallowed long and hard in that temperament. If it were not for the razor wire blocking him, Josephus would have broken into a sprint, scaled the fence, and evaporated into the known world. He couldn't, and in the processing of this revelation, he concentrated harder on each individual thump, careful to press sorrow into the low note while the high one reprieved, offering everybody in C Tier testimony on how a woman done him wrong.

Reality dictated that, soon, I too would get a Dear John letter from Beanie, who had been convicted and sentenced to eighteen months in Montgomery County. There was helplessness in the way Josephus banged misery, which receded as each minute elapsed. When the elegiac rhythm ceased, the slow drag boot heel of the nightshift guard replaced the vacated noise. She slowly made her rounds, pointing the flashlight into each cell to make sure everyone was present and accounted for. When the strong beam of light pierced into my cell, I was on the edge of my bunk with a rollup cigarette dangling from my lips.

In Roxbury, the options for inmate rehabilitation were limited. If an inmate did not have a high school diploma, he was required to attend GED classes until he passed the exam. There were trustee jobs like landscaping or working in the kitchen, which was a prized job. These workers had access to food, but more importantly, sugar, the most critical ingredient when making homemade wine or hooch. Sugar and cigarettes equaled dollar bills.

Another option was to take a computer workshop. Given my educational background, I had no problem securing a seat in the course, which consisted of working through a Microsoft Office tutorial with an instructor on site to answer questions. It was during this class that I met Old School, who had been incarcerated since 1952, when he was fourteen years old. When he first told me this, I had to mentally process what that meant in terms of history. He had missed the bombing of the Sixteenth Street Baptist Church, the assassinations of the Kennedys and Malcolm and Martin; he'd missed the political fervor of a nation. Old School had not raised his fist erect during the civil rights revolution, had remained clueless to what hip hop really meant, and "Yes, Yes Y'all" had no value to him at all. Crack and fiends crawling through the city at night in search of a white pebble might have been something overheard in conversation, but to him, really, it was make-believe.

Old School never told me his crime, and out of respect, I never asked, though to be locked up that long, the crime had to be murder. Incarcerated since before my birth, I came to know this man when time had become his enemy, the years producing too many body blows to the midsection. The first week we worked in Word, going over lesson plans that had us developing resumés and office correspondence like fax letters and memos. Old School sat next to me and asked questions every time we did a module. I didn't mind helping him because it was always good to have friends that had been in the joint that long. There was a certain respect for longevity behind bars.

During breaks, we went out to the breezeway and smoked Kite rollups. While inhaling menthol-flavored smoke, Old School always wanted to talk about the fear and terror trembling in his body. He did not know how to live a functional life on the outside and had become institutionalized, solely dependent on the state of Maryland to tell him what to do, how to do it, and when to do it. Old School understood he lacked any type of useful skill or vocation that would dictate his success in society. If it were not for the undeniable urge to pull a woman into the crook of his arms and run those needy fingers up and down her spine, he would gladly tell them to close the door—he ain't going nowhere. But the desire to breathe deep a woman's perfume helped propel him into the unknown that waited outside the gates of Roxbury.

In February, I received a letter from my lawyer informing me the request for a "modification of sentence" hearing had been approved. I also discovered that the prosecutor in the Nags Head case had dropped the charges because of too many continuances. Since my incarceration, Folks had been arrested in Fairfax, Virginia, because of information supplied by Connie about his activities regarding a string of burglaries in that county. Connie had disappeared and now had a warrant out for her arrest. Dealing with these factors for three years frustrated the prosecutor into dismissing the charges.

This was all good news, but there were still hurdles to clear. Later on that month, after hearing from my attorney, the opportunity presented itself for me to take a contemporary psychology course through Hagerstown Community College. The class met once a week in the prison and offered an opportunity to engage in something intellectual besides what went on in the dayroom and the computer shop.

There were twenty-five men in the class eager to learn the fundamentals of psychology. Having previous college credit was a prerequisite, and perhaps, in some small way, I wanted the class to be small to validate my own intellect. I wanted to believe I possessed something most inmates did not have—be it college or life experience. Perhaps I had constructed my own stereotype of an inmate, which was being shattered every day by guys like Black.

Black had not made it past the tenth grade, but for the past seven years had immersed himself in black nationalist literature, read books on theoretical and social constructs, and was one of the most intellectual debaters on race I'd ever met. At eleven, after final lock-in for the night, the guards allowed one inmate to push a makeshift cart around the housing unit to distribute ice to whomever wanted it. It was not only Black's job to push the cart around the cellblock, but he also considered it his human obligation to educate all who would listen. As he filled plastic cups and containers with ice cubes, I would stand by the metal door, with its small opening for a window, wrap my hands around the bars, and wait for the doors to slide back. Black called me "Black Man" as if to reiterate a fact I was not aware of. His dissection of the wretched implications of race almost always began with slavery and its inescapable connection to America—its present and perhaps its future. He performed salat without fail, always facing east. Religion, which he found through joining the Nation of Islam, taught him to read and write beyond what he would have ever done on his own.

One night while bringing around the ice cart to my cell, Black slipped a manila folder in my hand and said, "Read it carefully, Black Man." I took the manila folder and nodded my head.

Black had constructed a pamphlet of essays with two statistical tables on economic development in the Black community. It was only about thirty pages, but I was impressed at this juxtaposition of economics and community that examined how the lack of Black-owned businesses crippled our culture's growth. He laid out how, without economic power, Black folks would always be behind the eight ball, or, a better analogy, constantly pushing the boulder uphill like Sisyphus—a never-ending task.

The next morning in the day room, we had an intense conversation about his pamphlet. In every breath Black took, you could feel his commitment to giving something back to the Black community, if and when he got out of jail. At twenty-five years of age and only five years before his release, there remained a slim chance that he'd beat the odds and become a productive citizen. He and I were no different; we both faced the same statistical odds. The only way he knew how to climb out of his situation was to rail against and critique the very system that had placed him in jail.

Black came from dirt-poor East Baltimore. Never had nothing but what he got by hook or crook, and viewed drugs as the only viable way to obtain a modicum of success. It was always about the dollar-dollar-bill. Poverty began with his grandmother and continued with a mother strung out on heroin. Black's pamphlet asserted that this was the residue of a capitalistic society. It oppressed certain people and, at the same time, made those oppressed people feel like they had to emulate the oppressor in order to feel human. His family didn't have the education or fortitude to overcome this flawed system. He was also representing and processing a reoccurring trope within the black community in terms of the role of the father—as in, he didn't have one. Black was the darkest dude I have ever seen—blacker than a guy I grew up with in Birmingham who was so black he was blue—which was why we called him

Bluemeat. Bluemeat would have been Redbone next to Black.

We became fast friends through our engagement with language, with words and their cognitive meanings. We dissected everything in relationship to our own human condition, which spilled over into the psychology course I was taking. Black seemed to be interested in how the mind worked so he could use it to his advantage. After class, I usually returned to the housing unit and regurgitated the evening's lecture, waiting for his critique. We talked about dualism, which posited that the mind and body were two separate entities that came together to form a human experience. We talked about nature versus nurture as he tried to relate this concept to growing up in East Baltimore. Maybe he was a product of nature and the physicality of the streets. He questioned Western philosophy—in other words, he didn't trust white folks. His personal history with America allowed him to do anything but. Each day Black taught me a little more about myself and the way I had judged people like him all my life without ever noticing their substance.

The psychology course lasted six weeks and ended with my getting an A and three college credits. I kept trying to draw a contrast between the teacher and me. I wanted to be smarter than him, but he had the education, so I listened. I needed to learn what he knew. He had the book smarts, the degrees, a sense of self. Me having all the common sense got me nowhere, so I opened up my mind to a new way of thinking where I wasn't the center. What I took away most from the class were the conversations we had that ventured far from the course material, as everything got interpreted through the lens of the lives we were living. I was in a class with some of the state of Maryland's most hardened criminals—murderers, armed robbers, and rapists—philosophizing about life and the human condition. The teacher was so impressed with my work ethic and essays that he recommended I deliver a speech at the closing ceremony for inmates who completed the college class and any other programs like the GED and computer workshop. Hagerstown Community College would provide certificates of completion and bring in other speakers as well. Political officials within the community who wanted to see programming in prison would attend the event.

Sitting on the makeshift stage outside the prison chapel, waiting to deliver my speech, I kept reflecting back on Easter Sunday, 1973. Twelve years old and forgot my speech at Graymont Chapel African Methodist Episcopal Church. I had not taken the speech seriously, which, coupled with my slight stutter of the letters R and W, made me freeze stiffer than a Georgia pine in winter. I froze good and solid in front of a hundred Black folks who wanted to hear something about White Baby Jesus and kept staring straight through my eyeballs like I had committed the ultimate sin. I was petrified, and the fear in my body refused to allow the correct placement of articles, nouns, and verbs. I ran. I ran off the stage, ashamed.

But on this brittle April day, I grabbed the moment by the neck to articulate a speech on the importance of education that I wrote with the help of the blackest dude I know. I told the audience this moment in time could be a turning point. For a moment, my eyes locked with Old School, but I had no words to help him face the unknown. And there were many Old Schools in the audience. No one had an answer for them. Standing in front of that audience, I was ashamed I had squandered my potential. While becoming King of the Ghetto, I had become the King of Fools. No matter how smart I sounded on stage, I was still an inmate and convicted felon with a wretched past. I promised myself I would never be in this situation again.

After the ceremony concluded and I had nothing but time on my hands, I began to order university catalogues via mail. I examined course offerings and English majors, dreaming of the day I would be able to attend somebody's university full-time again. I wanted to study and to be a writer, although I had no clue how I would make a living. Education might be the only way to balance out multiple felony convictions. However, I could not begin the process if the court rejected my petition.

In three months, two plainclothes detectives who would have been spotted a mile away on any street corner I'd ever frequented would transport me back to Montgomery County Jail before daybreak. I would reside there in a cellblock for two more months before learning if a judge would grant me an alternative to incarceration.

My father is unequivocally 1970s. He is situated between Mexico City, 1968, and the hype surrounding two turntables spinning and back-spinning in a row house on 7th and S Streets in Northwest DC. I will forever remember him in cotton teardrop shirts like the ones he wore at Parker High School, where he taught Industrial Cooperative Training Monday through Friday, molding young boys and girls into something better than what they had come from. His pants were bell-bottomed, sometimes with a hard cuff breaking over a pair of Stacy Adams. He wore that old-time determination in his face, the hardness of his leathered skin telling how a boy climbed out of the barrel of poverty in Attalla, Alabama. There were so many obstacles, from not being allowed to cast a ballot to not being able to enter a restroom because he didn't fit the prescribed conditions stenciled on the wall. My father transcended these barriers while keeping that easy, sometimes hard-bop stride. The uncomplicated sway in his arms, the cool hip-talk of his speech—all of these things I admired.

I could not help but think of these traits in my father from behind that defendant's table in Montgomery County, inside an official-looking structure erected *for the good of the people.* The courthouse gallery contained a sparse number of citizens, mostly those waiting for loved ones to be brought from holding cells of iron and cement to meet their fates before the heavy-handed judge who was known for laying down the gavel—swift and relentless. The prosecution had just delivered a twenty-minute elocution on why I should not be given redemption. *Mr. Horton has had thirty-two years to get his life together, to prove he can be a productive member of society, and he failed that burden, Your Honor. We cannot simply allow him to roam free in our society. He deserves no second chance at freedom, no chance at a modification of his sentence.*

How to feel helpless when the mechanisms of justice want to lay a knockout right hook to your jaw. You're already punch-drunk from prison and its well-oiled machine. There's always one foot up your behind, so the rebellions you initiate only bring more grief, and somewhere in the middle of meditating in a six-by-nine-foot cell, seven days a week, three-sixty-five a year, the smell of men and their woes inescapable, there comes a revelation. Each night you interlock your fingers, place right palm over left palm—hands clasped in prayer—and you pray to a God. Although the origin of God is not clear, nor its gender or ethnic makeup, you just know there is something else out there greater than yourself. There has to be.

Before the prosecutor had justified his monthly salary, my attorney—the one the state gave as decoration—had failed miserably in her feeble attempt to convince the judge, or for that matter even me, why I should be let out of prison and given the opportunity to attend the Triangle Residential Option for Substance Abusers, or TROSA, in Durham, North Carolina.

But Dad was there for his boy. He made the two-hour flight from Birmingham to Washington National Airport, spent the thirty-five dollars for a cab to take him up Georgia Avenue to Rockville, and plopped down another eighty on a hotel room. That night he probably thought, *anything for my boy. I got to believe in my own seed. I mean, he come from me, hands like me, feet like me, face like me. He me. Can't leave my boy to rot in jail if there is something I can do or say. All a man's got is his family. How can I look at his momma knowing that I didn't give my all for her child, our child?*

He rose from the gallery of onlookers and passed through the swinging gate to take his place in front of the judge. Dad presented the last line of defense before I would surely be escorted back to Roxbury Correctional Institute to continue the process of rehabilitation. They would expect me to return to what most inmates do to rehabilitate themselves. I could do pull-ups from the stairs that descended from level two, and each pull-up, against gravity, could be the difference between the hole and lock-in: biceps bulging against all odds, lungs inhaling and exhaling, mind searching for a balance to the insanity that looms like a jaundiced wolf-eye over the prison.

Make no mistake, there is no rehabilitation of the mind. Time is merely a tourniquet squeezing and squeezing a man's brain until he's nothing but a *hum*. To escape this madness, I read books. Read books to condition myself against slipping into fragments, to re-emerge whole if ever given the chance. When a man goes to prison, he becomes a child in his sleep—every night a dream into the past—and through this portal, I was able to rediscover my father's constant message, how words are the ultimate power. I re-educated myself.

My father was my lone character witness. This was not a trial. That was done and over with. The boom laid down two and a half years ago. This was a response to a motion for reconsideration. Although the judge seemed indifferent to my lawyer's presentation for rehabilitation, my father was not deterred as he began to methodically outline the structure of my upbringing as a child. With stoicism, he spoke of the nurture and love I had received, even the presence of the leather strap and peach-tree braid switches. His speech described the Randall I had known long ago who had been lost to dimly lit street corners, intoxicated by the smell of evil that men do. From what my father said in an almost pleading voice, I had been respectful to others. I had displayed proper manners. I went to church every Sunday as a kid and had professed my life to the Lord and Savior Jesus Christ. I was even a steward and sat in the pulpit every third Sunday at Graymont Chapel AME. In school, I never quite measured up to my potential, but nonetheless made good grades. I had a mother and a sister who loved and supported me— even now in my darkest hour. I was ten classes short of a college degree. I had a foundation, a place to start from.

The voice began to crack under the enormity of the situation, the stance no longer as sure as it had started. He looked deep into the past, as if the words he wanted to say were hidden in magical compartments only he could see. My father began to waver, and I searched for saliva on my palate to swallow down my throat. I tried to erase my arms and legs, my body, and finally my face and eyes. It almost worked, too, except my ears could still hear the crack in his voice. He continued to break down, and my eyes opened back up, my body reappeared. I could see the moisture on his lids. He was talking about me, that third-person person whom I did not know anymore. The judge raised her face to my father's voice, her body leaning toward his plea, the ruggedness in her features relaxed. With everything his sixty-seven years had told him about people, my father searched for the compassion in her eyes. I wasn't me anymore. I was this reconfiguration of who he knew I could be. And finally he did it. My father placed his dignity before the court, and with teary rivulets coming steady now and his voice trying to stay proud, he begged the judge to give me another chance. *Please, please give me my boy back. His is a life worth saving.*

To feel smaller than nothing is probably not an accurate description of how I felt, but after nothing, what is there? Whatever it is, that's where my gut resided. Suddenly the persona I had orchestrated over many years was exposed for who he really was. This person I'm talking about had walked with a swagger of discontent and anger. He had seen his friends die and heard the Reaper knocking on his door more than once, trying to assure him that it was time to meet the maker. But he'd cheated the Reaper, too, because he was young and invincible. Except he was nothing but a fool who threw away love and didn't know how to get it back. The people on the streets whom he had called family were not here right now. *My* family was begging a stranger to set me free.

In front of a room full of strangers, my father cried. I looked around the room, and the people in the gallery were wiping their eyes. Women were opening their purses for tissue. The men were holding steadfast, afraid of doing the one thing in life they were taught not to do. My throat could not find any more spit. I wanted to choke myself and be done. Even my lawyer removed her glasses to clear them. The courtroom turned somber. The machine was human after all.

My father was quiet now, nothing left to give. He'd held sway inside the courtroom, given his all for his flesh and blood, the firstborn. He receded back through the swinging gate and took his place among the citizens in the gallery. In that moment, I put my face in the palms of my hands.

I rose to meet my destiny in front of the judge, who now looked taller than the pine trees back in Alabama when I was a little boy. I went from third-person periphery back to first-person me. I would be the one to receive this ruling. No persona could take my place.

She told me that I was the only one who put myself in this situation. Life was full of choices and decisions that can have an everlasting effect on the rest of our lives. There had to be order in a civilized society, with consequences for the most egregious offenses. She was moved, she said, by the passionate plea from my father. There was something here not to be taken lightly by the court. The fact that my father was in a courtroom, where fathers are notoriously absent, said a lot for what kind of family I came from and the possibility of a support system. I had served two and a half years of a five-year prison sentence. Think of what I was causing those closest to me to endure. I had not only gone to jail, but I'd taken my family, too. When she paused, I paused. My eyes followed her right hand. And then she swung the gavel down and said, *motion granted.* She collected herself, black robe and all, rose from the bench, and exited out the back door.

The holding cell was set up much like the one in Housing Unit III, C Tier in Roxbury, the shabby mattress thinly covered in green plastic and spread out on a slab of concrete, the gray cinderblock permeating a depression, the stainless-steel toilet and sink reflecting a dull shine that distorted your face when you stared into it.

Going home. The bailiff said *going home.* He had escorted me out of the courtroom back to the holding cell. Thirty years he'd been with the judge, watched her throw the book at people, refusing to grant an inch or any type of emphatic mercy. Mercy never happened. "That judge don't give out no favors," he said before he left. What happened was something special—he knew it and I knew it. I would not be going back to prison. I would never see my cellmate again. Processing would call my name soon. *Horton, bag and baggage.* The one phrase every inmate who sits in a cage wants to hear. Sweet music it is, sweeter than a soft note blown through the curvature of a saxophone. I would smell fresh air soon. But freedom came with a price—my father had shed his pride so that I might have a chance. *My boy, my boy—please save him.*

8

FEMALE PRISON

I've never been judgmental out loud, but I've had my own stereotypical ideas about people from the South. Television, movies, and books influenced those ideas. I've never traveled to the South much, but when I did, I was around fourteen. My sister, her husband, my niece, and I went to Virginia Beach. We did the bus thing. We traveled through all the cities before Virginia and slept in different hotels and motels. A few times, we came across people who weren't too friendly, but for the most part they were a lot kinder than New Yorkers. Up here, everyone has an attitude, and no one really gives a damn about the next person. I think that's why my parents always sent me away to Puerto Rico for the summer. They tried real hard to keep me away from the bullshit, but once I became a young adult, all I wanted to do was stay in the city for the summers and hang out.

I can understand why you felt the way you did about northerners; the swag is different, and some aspects of city folks are appealing, but home will always be where the heart is. I guess as a New Yorker, I have that same love for the city, but I have to admit there are times when I need to get away from the fast pace. I think that's what I loved most about Albany. It was far enough from the city, but close enough for me to get to. I know you hated Albany, but I kind of liked the peace and quiet. When I think about New York, I don't think I want to raise my son here. I want to raise him somewhere a li'l more slow-paced.

I think you are the only real friend I have from the South, and even though you have the smooth characteristics of a southern man, I think you've adopted a lot of the mannerisms and style of a New Yorker. I think we all adapt to our environment after a while, even if we try real hard to be resistant. I know I worked hard not to assimilate in Albany. I love my li'l Nuyorican accent, but sometimes the educated side of me takes over, and I can't help it—it often happens unconsciously. The girls here tease me about it, they say men must have a hard time dealing with me, and I guess they have a point. I think I'm getting more comfortable around you—well not literally, but you know, writing to you regularly. I like the fact you push me to think outside the box.

Last night I took my time reading the prison excerpts you sent. I made some coffee and found a nice spot on the rec deck and began reading. I was moved by the way you expressed yourself in the workshop at the detention center and how guilty you felt. It must have taken a lot out of you to pick up the phone and let your family know where you were after so much time had passed. Your journey of self-discovery began very bumpy. I mean, you definitely had your highs, but when you hit bottom, you were down there for a while, and I admire your come up. I wonder if you would be the same man had you not gone through those trials. It amazes me how you surrounded yourself in prison with people you admired, in even the smallest ways, and then took pieces of them with you when you walked back out into the world. I can see how much of Black rubbed off on you. In picking up the pieces of yourself, you were giving life to those who may never get a chance to live like real men and fulfill their dreams. I'm talking about men like that old-timer named Old School who spent most of his life in the clink.

In reading the excerpts about Roxbury, I realized the world of male prison is far different from female prison. I don't really have to worry about getting killed in here; these chicks in the feds are all a bunch of shit-talkers. They argue more than anything else, but they rarely throw hands. I had a rougher time in state prison because those chicks are a different animal altogether. In state, I got cut on my forehead with an Ajax top for defending a Puerto Rican girl who wanted to get *Blooded in*, and the *Blood* girls kept jumping her, so I fought the top girl. One of her goons passed her an Ajax top and she cut me slightly on the forehead, but I was getting at her good. I didn't get stitches. I asked the officer for salt and cleaned my wound and put pressure on it to stop the bleeding. I stayed in the bing for three months along with the girl who cut me behind that fight. They never bothered the Puerto Rican girl again.

Your experience in medium/max reminded me of mine at Albion and Bedford Hills. I was more nervous at Bedford than Albion because women in Bedford have mad time, and they don't give a fuck. In Albion, everyone had a date to go home and they all were a little bit more skeptical about starting trouble, but you still had bitches that didn't give a fuck about SHU and stayed on lockdown. In women's prison, it's more about jealousy and lesbians. If you're gay, then you and your partner are one, and it's a different rivalry, but if you're straight, all the gay women are trying to turn you out, and all of the femmes are jealous of you, trying to start rumors about you and every dyke and officer you talk to.

You once asked me, what do I think about the prison system, the death penalty, and how do I feel about people who have never been in prison who side with the death penalty and unconscionable laws. Well, Randall, I believe the average person who has never seen the inside of a cell doesn't fully understand how much the system breaks a person down. One can watch a ton of movies about jail and still not understand how this place fucks with your mind, your self-worth, and the way you interact with others. It's like you're trained to expect the worst, even if the person in front of you isn't capable of what you foresee. I don't know how to explain it, except that after my first jail experience, I was paranoid. That's why it's hard for me to swallow the fact that I'm here, but I know it's because I let a man get too comfortable in my space—something I hadn't done in years. I'd always kept home life separate, and this time I slipped because I was trying to be helpful. Now look at me; I walked right into a conspiracy.

Here's another thing that has me boggled about the system: the crimes don't fit the time. Why are people getting so much time for drugs while people with violent offenses receive far less? How come mules get bullshit charges and bullshit time, and conspiracy with intent to distribute holds a mandatory minimum of ten years? What people don't realize is, if we don't take the crazy plea deals the prosecuting attorneys offer, then the time more than triples if convicted at trial. We are caught in a no-win situation. Why is it that when you take a plea, you forfeit your rights to appeal and to put in motions? What happened to due process, and why is it that when people cooperate, the prosecutors always trump the charges? I really feel like prisons are a business more than a way to control society or the uncivilized of society. And how do they expect to reform people when once we come out it's hard to be accepted? I thought that by getting a degree and obtaining a job would be easier, but it wasn't—it was still difficult. I often had to work two jobs to subsist. How do they expect ex-cons to reintegrate into society when they are cast out?

Did you know when you apply for a job with the state, they tell you to apply as a disabled person because of your felony? When I first heard this, I was at the unemployment office in Albany,. The director of the office told me I had the right to apply as a disabled person because of the negative connotations associated with having a felony conviction. He said it would increase my chances at obtaining a state job because they have quotas that need to be filled.

In an effort to increase my chances at obtaining employment, I applied for a certificate of relief for civil disabilities only to be denied because I had a violent crime in my background, even though my role was not as the aggressor. It took a year for my paperwork to go before a tribunal, and I was shut down. The fact that I was tried and convicted as an adult before I was legally an adult is completely unfair. That should have been enough to grant me the certificate, but I was denied. I mean, how do they expect people who have been incarcerated to make it? The truth is, they don't. The system expects us to keep fuckin' up because they make money every time one of us comes back. And what is up with the three-strike scare? This is the stuff I'm talking about. How can you put a person away for life because they messed up three times—it doesn't make sense.

Then you have criminals, career criminals who have been arrested fifty- to sixty-plus times, and because they cooperate and rat other people out, they keep getting slaps on the wrist. The tactics used to manipulate people into talking are outrageous. The police will tell a criminal anything to get 'em to talk. I remember when I got arrested. It was only fifteen days after my surgery. I was still wearing that girdle, and I couldn't take it off for three months. I mean, really, I'd just had eight liters of fat sucked outta me and then like two liters shoved back into each butt cheek. I was in so much agony. Sitting was uncomfortable; lying down was uncomfortable; peeing, dressing, shitting—everything was uncomfortable. Have you ever been burned by a match on your finger? Well that's the sensation I felt all over my upper body. Can you believe those bastards wouldn't give me medication because they wanted to interrogate me first? They wouldn't even let me have Tylenol. I was on fire, and the authorities didn't give a fuck. The police wanted a hotel room number, and I didn't know it, so they kept pressing me. They put this form with the Miranda warnings and didn't let me check the last NO box until they were done pressing me for information. The detectives kept saying they had performed miracles for people in the past, that all I had to do was give them the hotel room number, but I really didn't know it. So they took me to the hospital after I passed out during interrogation. There I got served medication that would hold me over until I got to Rosie's on Rikers Island. Those bastards made me suffer. When I got to Rosie's, the prison officials thought I was strung out on heroin and treated me like a fiend. I didn't get any meds for days. To say I didn't have the strength to walk, eat, or shower would be an understatement. Just when I thought I was going to be released after three weeks of torture, the feds came and got me. Now, instead of facing eight years, I was facing ten to life, and here I am, still fighting for my freedom over drugs these motherfuckers know weren't mine.

Lxxxx

9

PRISON INDUSTRIAL COMPLEX

Dear Lxxxx,

Between Riverside Drive and the Henry Hudson, there is a one-way
side street running underneath silver-columned arches that hold
the curve of Riverside Bridge. Directly above, a dark gray ceiling
lulls the living. Sleepwalking through a series of "life" corridors,
the isolation suspends me in the continuum of time. Two red lights
dart straight at me, which means a white van is backing up, only to
discover no parking space. Above the elevated curve supported by
the silver arches, red block lettering moves silently across a screen
in reverse: THE WORLD IS A BETTER PLACE. Immediately, I dispel that
romanticism because, to the rest of the world, you are housed
within an invisible structure that most people choose to erase from
conscious thought. In five hundred years, the prison system is still
five hundred years behind. Lxxxx, the world cannot be a better place
if those who hold the keys fail to progress. We allow *caged mentality*
to exist on a large scale because we don't look for alternatives to
incarceration, and rehabilitation programs are virtually nonexistent.
If the structure is invisible, then so are you.

I've been thinking about what you wrote regarding prison,
and I'm processing these experiences in terms of my introduction
to *Tidal Basin Review's* Prison Industrial Complex Issue. I know—I
can't believe it has been a year since we've been writing back and
forth. Lxxxx, I know you understand that the idea of prison is
just that—an idea, not tangible to most people in society. If the
structure doesn't affect you, then how will you notice it? In our quest
to become human, we eliminated slavery, outlawed lynching and
other barbaric acts, yet we can't stop prison from being a training
ground for more and worse crimes. The short version: capitalism
and Republican legislators created the War on Drugs in the '80s
via legislation that began during the Civil Rights Movement, which
gave us the prison industrial complex, built on gross misuses of the
Fourth Amendment. During the implementation of the Reagan laws,
crime was actually receding. The machine of big business and right-
wing conservative views did not benefit the proletariat, and neither
did the drug laws, where race tipped the scales. These laws only came
about because drugs began to infiltrate suburban white America.
Well-to-do kids were getting strung out on dope, caught in urban
ghettoes trying to score, and subsequently mugged or shot.

The addicted suburbanite came as a residual of the crack
epidemic, and somebody had to pay for the disgrace. Getting caught

with an ounce of hard became a ten-year mandatory minimum, while an ounce of powder garnered probation or minimal time. Let's call this Economics 101. In the urban centers of the economically deprived, you get soft (powder) to make hard (crack), or you already get it hard; nobody buying soft like that. Vials littering the street: red cap, blue cap, yellow cap. White folk came from the countryside into the city for crack. Forget about what you heard. These laws were meant to preserve a way of life. Get them niggas, spics, wops, and wetbacks who are poisoning the good upstanding white off the street. See, it's one thing when we killing ourselves; it is another thing to inflict pain on the dominant social structure: the bourgeoisie, them folks who can't even see you. The Reagan era built its foundation on the fallacy of rising prison numbers leading to sinking crime, and the people bought it hook, line, and sinker.

The prison system began as a way to balance crime with consequence. This consequence means more to the person doing the imprisoning than the prisoner him or herself. Going back to Nietzsche, his "aristocrat" would be our upper middle class needing to validate its own worth so it can exist on a higher plane than (us) the proletariat. I present this example, where Nietzsche writes, *Much rather has it been the good themselves, that is, the aristocratic, the powerful, the high-stationed, the high-minded, who have felt that they themselves were good, and that their actions were good, that is to say of the first order, in contradistinction to all the low.* The ones who created the scared were now scared of the low. The Reagan laws fit within this rubric. The laws were to protect those deemed good through their wealth and economic position while ignoring the underlining psychosis of the problem: lack of generational wealth and institutionalized racism. No one notices that invisible sign.

R

JOURNAL NOTE TO [SELF]:
BURN THE HOUSE

Steadfast summer disintegrates into the nonchalant winds of October, each day demanding that the body become more aware of clothing wrapped around complicated flesh. Melodies of aureate and auburn cling to verdant leaves fluttering amidst the gray horizon, juxtaposed against neocolonial structures of brick and mortar geometrically designed in the city, where humans sell themselves, around a clock with no hands, to a sort of inescapable commodification. Inhalation is a little crisper, the change of alphabets electrifying the body and, consequently, the mind—perhaps a new way of thinking—and so walking down 125TH STREET begins the soundtrack: between turntables angelic without angel wings, the deejay. Sound controlled by pitch, speed—cut.

Kneel in prayer, *Ode to the Proletariat*, when the music stops, but until then, the crowd works to a sweat frenzy. *Somebody scream*, out of the speakers comes *the common came to scream*, and then: loud. Elbow crooked over the Technics (yo, check the technique). Ear pressed to headphone, fingertips feeling the black wax groove, and then, stop—crossfade. Somebody, *sheeeit, oh yeah*. Everybody all in—vibrating bone, a collage of music becoming a collage of bodies, multihued explosions of color into no color, a chromatic drone *humming* parallel to sight. Coming out of the music back to 125TH STREET inside the throng crossing Lenox, this imagistic constraint inside the brain performs a conjured ideal, accumulated over time, through memory. Every hole in the wall, every basement party, every deejay battle runs concurrent to what is heard/seen/remembered. Perhaps we imagine through culminating experiences. *Oh yeah*, is the loop repeated in my head. *The roof!* in my head is what I remember, the drummer still beating in my head: *we don't need no water let the muthafucka burn!*

MAIL CALL: LXXXX PXXXX
INMATE NUMBER (37XXXXXX)
FEDERAL DETENTION CENTER
PO BOX 329002
BROOKLYN, NY 11232

TROSA, 2000

TROSA did not operate under the basic assumptions of atonement, but instead confronted the drug problem based on how strong a work ethic one could develop while being held accountable for unacceptable behavior. TROSA took the worst drug addicts—the ones in and out of jail, the ones familiar with a street gutter, the dope mainliners, the cocaine inhalers, the fiends snatching presents from under the Christmas tree before the big day. The men and women coming to TROSA could admit they were powerless over addiction in one breath and by nighttime be on a full-fledged coke binge, carousing in dope dens and targeting who to jack. TROSA believed in shock therapy, as in cussing a muthafucka out on the spot about dope-fiend behavior. Nice didn't work, so *fuck you* was the only option.

When released from prison, the courts permitted me to travel to my sister's house in Augusta, Georgia for Christmas. They granted me ten days of unsupervised freedom, and then I needed to report to Durham. Because of my years in prison and my absence from our family before, my sister's family Christmas traditions were all new to me. My nieces did not recognize the uncle they'd heard talked about more than they'd seen. Camren, the youngest, had only met me when she was a newborn. Sydney, the oldest, knew me when she was two, but didn't remember what I looked like. I had become an invisible man in their eyes, words more than flesh, only rendered tangible when I showed up from prison. It felt good to be around family. My mother had visited me once, before I went upstate to Hagerstown. I had not seen my father since the courtroom hearing. Now there wasn't any thick glass or partition or black phone to pick up from its cradle to conduct a conversation. The prodigal son had returned, beaten up by the streets, broken by prison. That night, on the kitchen table covered in newspaper, there were crab legs sprinkled with Old Bay Seasoning, Italian sausage cut into quarters, red potatoes, corn on the cob, cornbread made from a cast iron skillet, boiled shrimp. Christmas was good.

Riding the Greyhound to Durham from Augusta, I felt so much apprehension for my new surroundings. The visit with my family only further solidified my guilt at having let them down by going to prison. While my mother and father welcomed me with open arms, I knew that, deep in the backs of their minds, they privately wondered if I would be able to stay out of jail. I didn't realize how important family was until I blocked them out of my life. But more than that, I would not be returning to Housing Unit II, C Tier, Cell 16 to talk with Black or relish in the memory of Old School's dread about an ever-changing world. My mother, father, sister, brother-in-law, and two nieces would not see me for at least a year, and I would not be able to leave TROSA until I completed twenty-four months. Since I came court-ordered, any infraction or violation of the program's rules and regulations would immediately send me back to Maryland's state prison system.

TROSA didn't pay compensation to the residents of its facility and enjoyed 501(c) nonprofit status. Call it free legal labor. Its moving company alone generated over three million dollars a year. Besides T-West, there was T-North, which functioned as the central housing unit for people ordered to the program, as well as T-East, which operated as a warehouse and storage facility. For thirty days, residents stayed in the converted middle school that was T-North. They slept in the gymnasium on cots and rose at five to serve breakfast, clean up, and go to work. They would be expected to come back after work and serve dinner, clean the kitchen, wipe down walls, mop floors, and basically do grunt work.

While on the moving crew, I learned to pack dishes and wardrobe boxes, as well as wrap flat-screen televisions and load a twenty-four-foot truck. Every night we residents looked on a board located on the first floor in T-North to see what our assignment would be for the next day as determined by a dispatcher in the moving office. When we arrived at T-West in the mornings, we knew whose truck we would be riding in the back of and who the crew boss would be. The work was physically demanding, and if that didn't break you down, then the rules and regulations would bend you almost to submission. There would be no correspondence by mail for the first thirty days. No phone calls for ninety days. No talking to females for one hundred eighty days. No home visits for one year, and then only escorted until you reached eighteen months in the program. Everything was determined through a milestone.

TROSA prohibited calling home for three months because they didn't want anyone to feel homesick and walk away. Two months into the program, I was assigned to a crew that would be performing contract labor at IBM in the Research Triangle area. Twenty-five offices needed to be moved to another building, and the job would probably last all day. The telephone stared at me from in the middle office, begging to be dialed. When my mother answered the phone, surprised I would be calling home this early in the program, I sensed apprehension in her voice. She then proceeded to inform me my father had been diagnosed with prostate cancer. I could only ask, *Is he gonna be okay?* Taking the phone from my mother, my father explained the diagnosis came early, and a full recovery was expected. Somehow *cancer* negated anything he said. To me cancer equated to death.

Since I shouldn't have used the phone on the job site, I dealt with the news internally, each day going through the motions of the program while worrying about my father's health. A month later, I received a letter from my mother explaining that the operation had been a success, and there should be a full recovery. The news enabled me to concentrate on leaving TROSA and resuming my life. After six months of riding on the back of a moving truck, the administrators elevated me to the title of dispatcher. I had disclosed my educational and work background during intake, and the administrators felt I would be a good fit. Since my supervisor could not see the front of my monitor, I began to write poems in chaos: a phone ring, the cursing out of someone who screwed up on a job assignment—noise all around.

I was now in conversation with the poet E. Ethelbert Miller. He worked at Howard as the Director of the African American Resource Center. I first contacted Ethelbert after reading a front-page profile of him in a copy of *the Washington Post* that someone had left in TROSA's dayroom. I told Ethelbert I would gladly clean up bathrooms in Douglass Hall for a chance to return to Howard University, atone for my mistakes, and finish what I'd started. I regretted having blown such an opportunity. I didn't understand how important education was until I could not obtain it. Now I understood. He wrote back and told me his influence on admissions and scholarships had limits; however, he would keep an eye out for opportunities. I sent him my poems, and he responded with feedback and suggestions. I was so grateful for his guidance. At night, in T-North's dorm area for men, I practiced reciting poems, hoping one day I would get the chance to perform on HBO's *Def Poetry Jam* like I'd seen Patricia Smith and Saul Williams do.

After having been there a year and wanting desperately to learn all I could about poetry, I saw Samantha Thornhill as a featured poet in Hillsborough, North Carolina, at a cafe called Vague Metaphors. I was enamored of her attention to lyrical cadence, her command of imagery, and a disposition that spoke to her living her life's passion through poetry. However, what caught my attention most was when she mentioned she was getting an MFA in creative writing with an emphasis in poetry from the University of Virginia, and that the former United States Poet Laureate Rita Dove was mentoring her.

Samantha did not shake my hand or talk to me that night because I was too self-conscious about my own inadequacies as a poet to introduce myself. But more than that, she did not know that I had been at Triangle Residential Options for Substance Abusers for twelve months and was being escorted by one of the counselors in the program to her reading.

When I hit the twenty-one-month mark, I went on workout and secured a job at Carolina Odds & Ends, which often temporarily hired TROSA people for Thanksgiving and Christmas. During the same time period, the program allowed and paid for me to take a world literature class at North Carolina Central. I began to feel as if, finally, I was making progress. The class met twice a week, and I got to converse with students, which allowed me to have contact with the world outside of TROSA. Going into the class, I was apprehensive and wondered how the students would perceive me. It took a couple weeks to open up and join discussions because I was afraid I would say something wrong, something that revealed my time in prison. I only told the professor my situation, and he was very supportive. He even agreed to write a letter of recommendation to Howard, which was my ultimate goal destination. Through constant study and the writing of poetry, my analytical and thinking skills improved. The literature class taught me to examine situations for the deeper meaning, the metaphor, to understand history and how my life's narrative intersected with the world's condition.

My father disagreed with the idea of my returning to DC after prison and a drug program because—as any rational person might—he summed up the fragmented parts of my past experiences and made a logical deduction that Washington, DC, should not be my home anytime within the next millennium. However, I knew I needed to accomplish something in Washington in order to move forward. Going to Howard and finishing my degree was the goal. I felt that any other act on my part would constitute running away from the problem, and I'd been running away from things full speed all my life. At thirty-eight years of age, incarceration and failure could not be the crowning achievements of over twenty years spent in DC. My father's concerns were genuine and valid. Temptation and old friends would be loitering around every corner. There would be an inner voice always speaking, like the siren of a crack pipe calling its long-lost offspring back into the fold, to return to the misery. But I wanted—no, needed—to escape. And I would.

My parents attended a historically black university because they had no choice; the word SEGREGATED did not permit them to dream of an integrated college. Alabama A&M University allowed both to acquire undergraduate and graduate degrees in education and become secondary education schoolteachers. My parents exuded immense pride in their college, attending football games, displaying alumni spirit, and I wanted to be part of such a legacy, as well.

Returning from prison and a two-year stay at a drug program, I applied to be readmitted to Howard as a returning student. The rejection letter came via snail mail. Because I had been convicted of seven felonies, Howard reported their institution would not be able to readmit me at this time. The interpretation between the lines seemed to say:

> Nigga, what you think this is? We's upstanding good-ass knee-grows 'round here. Can't let dead weight like you bring down de entire race. Boy, don't you know you life over? We only want de best and brightest. Hoodlums like you set knee-grows back fitty years. Must be out you damn mind if you think we gone let your criminal-convict ass up in here. Nigga please. You had a chance but fucked it up. Tough. That's life. Suck it up.
> Signed Sincerely,
> The Knew Knee-Grows

The school thanked me for my interest in returning before wishing me good luck (*fuck you, nigga*). This is how dreams derail and have to right themselves if to continue. Everyone from the prosecutor to the Mecca of Black Institutions wanted to count me out, to place the nail in the coffin even before my death, as in *bury me alive*. I did not possess the luxury of wasting time, so I enrolled at the University of the District of Columbia in the spring of 2003. The school welcomed me unconditionally to their English Department, and the dream continued.

From the time I returned to the time I left DC, I worked at Metropolitan Towing in Arlington as a dispatcher because no one else would hire me. Unemployment doors slammed often and without remorse. Every time I applied for a job, the rejection came shortly after. Working as a dispatcher was a job I had experience in coming from TROSA, and even though most companies told me no, Metropolitan Towing said yes when I interviewed in their small, single-wide trailer converted into a dispatch office, complete with bulletproof glass.

Extended from the trailer was the tow lot encased in a chain-link fence. The actual dispatch office only had a computer and a desk with limited space. Customers could not enter the trailer. There was a makeshift hutch built with a small four-by-four-foot space for customers to enter and transact business. Employees had to come through the electronic gate and enter through the back. Ms. Lee, a Korean woman in her early sixties, told me the job didn't pay much, but I could log overtime hours and work my schedule around my classes. The felonies were never an issue during the interview. The first night, it became evident why perhaps having been to prison might be a benefit.

Training came by way of a bald Puerto Rican kid named José, along with Mr. Lee—no relation to Ms. Lee but nonetheless a Lee and an owner—who was in the back room counting the day's receipts, eating kimchi, and sipping brown liquor in a shot glass with the door closed. Not even an hour passed when in walked a family of four, who had paid their food bill at a nearby restaurant only to exit into March's late night breeze to discover that their late-model Audi had vanished. This is where the bulletproof glass comes into play—it's a necessary barrier. People were never excited to get their car towed, and that was also true of this well-to-do family, which I deduced from the lavish mink coat on the mother, the expensive pearls on the daughter, the camelhair London Fog on the father, and the son's Philly fade cut with a part on the side. After following the directions on the sign that read, IF YOUR CAR GETS TOWED CALL THIS NUMBER and paying twenty dollars for a cab, the father demanded to know where the fuck his car was. In moments of rage, the bourgeois façade is the first to go.

José grabbed the ticket from the wooden file box and shouted through the hole in the glass, "Parked on the white line. See picture. On the line." I was standing right behind José since I was supposed to be in training.

"You can't be motherfuckin' serious," the mother said, her lavish mink coat all pomp and show.

José replied, "Yeah," bringing a miniature baseball bat from under the counter, which I didn't understand since we were behind thick glass and they were in the hutch.

The patriarch of the family began to curse José. Both Mink Coat and Pearls joined in the fray, mouthing a chorus of *fuck yous*. Three voices I counted, but four bodies had entered through the hutch. I looked out the back window and noticed that the last driver had left the gate open. Then I saw that the son—much bigger and stronger, a larger carbon copy of his father—had exited the makeshift entrance for customers and slipped in through the gate. He bolted up the steps to our part of the single-wide, opened the door, and lunged for José. I stepped to the side.

The son and José battled it out in the limited space of the office, making every thrust, push, tug, and pull harder to actualize. They negotiated spaces around and in between me while I searched for a way out of the trailer, as this was not my fight. Mr. Lee ran out from the back to defuse the situation, but his erratic shouts made matters worse. The son released José and grabbed Mr. Lee's neck. Again, I stepped to the side. Mr. Lee's broken English devolved into gurgles and gasps for precious air. José tried to gain balance, but at that moment, the father barreled in through the door, knocking him onto the floor in the back office. Not sure who called the police, but someone called. Sirens and flashing lights forced everyone in the trailer to freeze before the police had even uttered a word. This was day one.

Working at the towing company and drawing a paycheck allowed me to settle back into the city and concentrate on graduating from UDC with a degree in English. Because most of the people I had associated with before prison had bets on how long I would last on probation, I stayed clear of my past, except for Craig. After about a year, I sought him out because he was wrestling with a heroin habit and had fallen hard. His dad was now in prison serving double life, and the pipeline of drugs, which at one time seemed to never end, had now dried up. One night, Craig stopped by my studio apartment in need of a place to crash. I let him grab the couch for as long as he needed. Soon after, I got him a job working at the tow company.

I could not knowingly turn my back on a friend I'd known for years. Many times, he'd looked out for me, helping me survive in the drug world. Craig still got high, but I asked him not to do it around me, and he did not. Maybe I was a facilitator to his misery by letting him grab the couch, but what else could I have done? I knew homelessness firsthand, and seeing Craig in this state helped me understand I could never return to the life I had left.

Going to school, working, and concentrating on poetry

became my main focus, while trying to avoid old friends and associations who would try to pull me away from the life I wanted. Shortly after coming back to DC, I began to frequent a café called Teaism, an official venue for the National Poetry Slam. I loved the performance aspect of poetry and became DC Slam Champion in 2004, but I felt my craft and language needed to grow. I needed a foundation to actually study poetry in a concentrated way. Although Howard did not readmit me, I unofficially audited a creative writing workshop with the poet Tony Medina, who welcomed writers from the community at large. I was taking the class right up under the Knew Knee-Grows' noses through UDC's consortium agreement with Howard. In many ways, I looked at being on campus as a way to continue to understand my mistakes, to realize how bad I had fucked up when I entered that school back in 1979. Each time I walked on the yard to go to class, I knew the rejection letter existed, that I wasn't really welcome.

Medina knew I had been incarcerated, so I later often wondered if, when he handed me *The Essential Etheridge Knight* and turned to "Feeling Fucked Up," he understood the connection I would feel toward another poet who had shared the prison experience—and written about it. I read the poem aloud and wondered, who was this poet talking about *fuck Coltrane and music and clouds drifting in the sky?* The poem spoke to me as if I had written it. *The Essential Etheridge Knight* taught me to speak about erasure, because I do not come from the language of clouds drifting in the sky. I do not come from the white dogwood bloom and purple lilac of spring. I come from the tornado swirl of a crack pipe, from the click-clack of Little Lulu's red boots dragging sidewalk down Rhode Island Avenue. In reading Etheridge, I began to understand how I would situate myself not only within the black tradition of writing, but the entire scope of American Letters. Etheridge gave me a blueprint from the back alleys and prisons to the page.

In the spring of 2004, my academic advisor informed me that I would be able to graduate from UDC in the fall with a BA in English. I began to think of graduate school as a possibility. Then a knock on the door came around 10:00 a.m. on a Tuesday. The incessant banging did not stop until I pulled the front door open to a muscular man with US MARSHALL on his windbreaker. A badge in one hand, an official-looking paper in the other. Mr. US MARSHALL read, *Randall Horton, we have a warrant for your arrest for failure to appear in Alexandria County, Virginia, in 1998.*

Unlocking the deadbolt, I rolodexed through the past decade of my life, trying to remember the circumstances around this situation. Then too, I wondered how was it possible to go through a prison system, be released, get sent to a two-year drug program, graduate from said program, damn near complete eighteen months of probation—basically have my name run through every database in the United States of America—without one regulating authority informing me of a warrant for my arrest? Trying to explain to MR. US MARSHALL never does any good, so I turned and assumed the position I knew well: spread eagle, hands behind the back. Out the apartment, into the unmarked car.

Riding across the 14th Street Bridge from DC to Alexandria in mid-April, one first encounters the cherry blossoms in full bloom along the streets, then the dark blue sheet of water rolling into Virginia. Taking in the Potomac River, I was scared, scared I might be going back to prison. So far. I had come so far, and now the past was tapping me on the shoulder, saying *hold up, wait a minute, jack.* I could hear that old Knew-Knee-Grow voice in my inner ear, again:

> Dumb nigga,
> Said ya wouldn't neva be nothing. Bottom of de barrel. Dats what ya is. Bottom of de barrel convict. Spell it: C-O-N-V-I-C-T. Statistic, a sad sad statistic. De Knee-Grow race gotta keep moving, and de human race don't need you, will never accept ya, even if you snuck in a class. Fucked ya life up and now ya want a li'l empathy to rise above ya circumstance? Fall nigga. Fall back into the gutter you wallowed in. Can't do nothing but keep us down. Down. Down. Down. As always, us still a li'l Sambo. No Booker T. Washington "cast down your bucket" here.
> Sincerely Yours,
> The Knew Knee-Grows

By the time I was fingerprinted, booked, and classified, the magistrate had been called away on an important matter and would not return until morning, which meant I would not receive a bond until then. The holding cell reeked of urine and dry concrete. I sat cross-legged on the floor on a flimsy green mattress because I could not find anywhere else to sit. The lump of human flesh under a gray wool blanket in the corner smelled of cheap whiskey and stale cigarettes— and snored loud and long.

The deputy came to the door, unlocked and rolled it back, then handed me a piece of paper explaining the charges in detail. Before Montgomery County and Hagerstown, I'd done time in Fairfax, Virginia, for a series of laptop thefts. Consequently, Alexandria came calling for a crime committed in 1996 when a person or persons unknown broke and entered into a computer store in an obscure retail plaza hidden from the main road, which is US Route 1. The morning store manger had unlocked the deadbolt and disengaged the alarm only to find that it would need to be sounded after all because there were no computers to sell. The store looked as if someone was moving in—or perhaps out. This is what the prosecuting attorney told my court-appointed lawyer in 1997. In return, my lawyer retorted or, more specifically, stated: *Let it be known that no fingerprints were found. No surveillance camera to record the theft, nor any eyewitnesses,* which in a court of law means dismissal. No evidence, no case.

However, the prosecutor persevered and offered a three-year plea bargain to run consecutive to my time in Fairfax. My lawyer suggested we go to trial, and I agreed. We decided to rock instead of cop. Minutes before trial was to begin my lawyer came to the holding cell and informed me the prosecutor had moved for *nolle prosequi* on the case. This meant that charges had been dropped with the option to revisit if other evidence surfaced. I left the next day, back to Fairfax County to finish an eighteen-month bid.

Evidently, when I had returned to Fairfax, the prosecuting attorney had re-filed the case. No one informed my lawyer or me. No one tried to locate me in prison, and so I slipped through the system, which is what I told my father when he picked up the phone and heard, *You have a collect call from an inmate at the Alexandria County Detention Center.*

The call scared him more than anything. *Shit,* he mumbled into the receiver. But after he accepted the call and I gave him the story, he seemed mildly relieved that I was not locked up for some present offense. Walls closing in—fast. Couldn't breathe. Boundaries—again. To the left, the right, behind, even overhead— limitations as to where I could and could not go. The cell shrank until it became part of my bones—again.

All night long, no sleep. The lump snoring under the blanket, the chatter from the guards outside my cell, even the piss smell kept me up wondering what kind of new evidence had been found. What if I had to do the time? Could I handle it again? When do you stop reaping what you sow?

The next morning, I was given a ten thousand dollar bond and released. Ms. Lee put up the bond money because she trusted and needed me to dispatch during the day. Because I had a good command of the English language coupled with office and communication skills, she and Mr. Lee often depended on me to deal with new contract clients. The thousand dollars—ten percent of ten—would be taken out of my check bit by bit.

Since I did not want to chance a public defender with my future, the lawyer handling my case was E. Douglas Ellis, Attorney-at-Law. Three years older than me, he had attended the same high school that I had, and eventually Howard as well. Doug was a friend of the family, and I needed to call on him to make sure I did not go back to jail. He sorted out the specifics of my case, then asked for and got a continuance at the first trial date. The first-degree burglary case carried a sentence of up to twenty years. Turns out that, after some probing, attorney E. Douglas Ellis came to the discovery that no eyewitnesses nor fingerprints—no evidence—had surfaced in almost seven years, and since I was not going to snitch on myself, E. Douglas Ellis persuaded the prosecution to drop the case again.

The path to graduation cleared ahead of me. While waiting on the outcome of my case, I had traveled with Tony Medina's class to the second Furious Flower at James Madison University, which is a conference that honors African American poetry. There I ate dinner with Amiri Baraka and met a host of other writers like Haki Madhubuti, Lucille Clifton, and Sonia Sanchez. I left the conference encouraged by these literary giants. Having my case dismissed was a huge relief. I could now pursue my dream of getting an MFA, just like Samantha Thornhill, the poet I had seen in North Carolina who let me know that a life as a poet was possible.

Not too far from the Appalachian foothills, this pristine valley is like prayer. My father grew up in this complex region, so I feel an innate connection to the land, to the mountains, to the lake, and to the eagles that return every year to mate. In November, I received word I had been selected as a National Endowment for the Arts Fellow in Literature. Our quiet moment of celebration was spent fishing under the bridge on the stone banks of Lake Guntersville about a foot from the riverbed, waiting for a red-and-white cork to bob so we could reel in the crappie. We talked about what it meant to be honored by my peers with this award and how I had progressed since incarceration. The conversation switched for a moment to a young kid named Love who had come by my office at the University of New Haven, where I now taught.

Love was just getting out of prison. Bill, one of his mentors, had read an article about me in the *New Haven Register*. He called and asked if I would talk to Love about the difficulties of staying out of prison and negotiating life with felonies. Love was at that same age at which I had begun to derail my own journey in life. I explained to my father how our lives were intertwined, and that prison bound Love and me in a way most people would never understand, yet we were different insofar as he came from a broken home. I did not. I had a father in my life. He did not.

My father continued to bait his hook, careful to peg the minnow just under the belly, closer to the tail, and I shared Bill's letter with him.

> Dear Dr. Horton,
> It would take a poet to find the right words to express my gratitude to you for meeting on Friday with Love and me. The meeting was one of the bright and shining high points of Love's life. I looked over at him several times during the meeting, and he was mesmerized, rapt, literally on the edge of his chair, drinking in every word. He talked about you and about the meeting all the way home. He had met another poet! A poet who had his poems in books! He kept checking on his memories of what you had told him during the meeting to make sure he had not misunderstood. "He said he was in prison, right? He said he started writing poetry when he was in that

program that the judge sent him to, right? He was like a slam champion, right? Damn, that cool. Some of the books he give me, they be poems by other Black poets, right? He teach at that college and he said I can go to his class next year, right?" He was exhilarated, as was I. He couldn't wait to tell his mom and siblings. I kept thinking to myself, I have just witnessed great acts of pure kindness and selfless giving, and just to witness that is a gift in itself. I think Love had the same reaction, but couched in his history, it came out as a question: "Why he do all this for me, he don't even know me?" All I could do was remind him that you had said that there were people who had helped you along the way, and you wanted to give back. I think Love gets that.

I talked to him this evening on the phone, and he was still flying pretty high! He told me that his mom cried when she heard about the meeting and saw the books; his sister was pissed off that he could go to a college course even if he hadn't finished his GED when she did have to finish her GED; and his aunt didn't believe that he had met the man who wrote one of the books you gave him! And he asked me if I would write to you to say thank you from him since it takes a while for him to write things and he doesn't know where to mail it. I told him I would, and that I also would get him your address so that, no matter how long it takes, he can write to you himself.

So, thanks from Love for the meeting, for the inspiration, for the story of your journey, for the understanding, for the books, and for the offer to have him attend your class next semester. And thanks from me for all of the above and for the opportunity to watch this unfold. I hope the closing on your house went without a hitch. By the way, if you will be moving furniture into your new house on your own, let me know. I'll recruit Love and we'll come over with my pickup truck to give you a hand. Be well, and I'll keep in touch.
Best,
Bill

My father and I were under a bridge that supports the same highway toward Birmingham that he had sped down after work in the middle of the night on October 16, 1961, upon hearing of my premature birth at three in the morning. He had taken a job over an hour away from his pregnant wife to support his growing family. In these moments that follow, we are teacher and student, even if he doesn't say a word. This day, there is a chill in the air that should not be present in April in the South. Dogwoods have not bloomed, and herein resides the problem of no fish—as in we haven't caught nothing all morning. The fishing gods prophesize that, when dogwoods bloom in April, crappie literally jump out of the water and onto the hook. But I'm not thinking about the chill or the lack of fish or the hook—only reveling in the space between us. In the silence, I want to spill out little pieces of memory to my father, to tell him about near-death escapades—of being held at gunpoint, or participating in a murder that never happened.

Midday, and the lake's current flows calm while mallards drift under the bridge toward us, occasionally dipping their calcium beaks below the surface. One lone bass jumps out and back into the dark water, and then vanishes. Overhead, I can't help but note that there is something graceful about an eagle being able to spread its wings, the arc of motion in the expansive sky spelling something like freedom, and how to watch this superior display of intelligent life is daunting—you could even call it gangster, knowing that this bird is the envy of humans who have, since the beginning of time, claimed freedom as the ultimate sign of humanity. But I know that arms are not wings and that we are earthbound by the gravity of the living. We want to know the high that blares through the eagle's nostrils, the way she rounds into the evening sun, motionless, if only for a moment. I remember that high.

After another hour, we pack our tackle and leave to visit John El, one of my father's oldest living relatives at ninety.

When I was enrolled in the MFA program at Chicago State University, John El's detailed knowledge of a shootout in 1912 had provided the backstory for my thesis and first poetry book, *The Definition of Place*. At the time, I was living in Chicago in a small, cramped studio apartment in Hyde Park. When I heard my dad say, *covered wagon*, I muted the television. and I asked him to repeat what he had said.

"There was a shootout in a covered wagon. The Fennels, your cousins on my momma's side, were coming home from church and were attacked by two white men. Your Great-Great Granduncle Bud and Uncle Dennis came over the ridge about the same time, and that's when the shootout happened."

"How come I never heard about this?"

"Talked to John El and he reminded me the other day. Killing those white men was the family secret no one ever talked about. John El heard the story from his mother as a little boy. I heard about it when I was child, too, but we never talked about it. You have to remember that in 1912, killing a white man meant hanging from a rope. And 1938 wasn't much better, either. Sometimes you keep secrets silent so long they become forgotten."

The conversation led me to discover that my grandfather, Elvie Horton, had gone to jail in 1930 during the Great Depression for distilling moonshine in the back hills of Alabama. My maternal grandmother's brother, Uncle Sydney, received a dishonorable discharge for killing a black man during World War II in Australia. Because Sydney was black as well, no further charges were filed. Upon his return to US soil, Sydney then promptly decapitated his wife when he assumed her to be cheating. Sydney's other sister, Emma, who lived on the South Side of Chicago and ran an after-hours joint, drove ten hours in a chauffeured black Packard complete with running boards to bribe the authorities for a reduced prison sentence. Sydney then escaped while working on the chain gang in Northern Alabama and swam the rugged Tennessee River to Chicago in a mad dash. While in Chicago, I began taking trips to interview John El, who proved invaluable during the research phase of *The Definition of Place.*

Today, we ride in silence to see John El, and I can't help but wonder what it was like for my dad growing up in the Deep South during segregation. How did incarceration skip him and not me? And while the eagles had returned to reaffirm life, my father and I had returned also—to the red clay, to the dirt from which we are all born.

10

ONE MORE THING

DEAR RANDALL,

I've started so many letters to you, and I never finish. It's not because I'm lazy; I just want my letters to be neat and coherent. A part of me feels like I told you too much, and even though you asked me, maybe you didn't expect me to be open and honest. I apologize if I made you feel guilty for asking me to share my past with you—that wasn't my intention. I trust you and I'm not ashamed to bear it all. Something deep inside lets me know that, regardless of what I tell you, you wouldn't judge me. When I received the bell hooks book that you sent me, *All About Love*, I started reading it immediately, and the lady blew me away. She helped me look at love differently—with understanding. I've always known the type of love I've experienced and witnessed in my life had to be twisted, but she explained why, and it made perfect sense. All I've ever seen in my life is abuse. I grew up in a dysfunctional household—but then again, who didn't? What is a normal household? One thing's for certain, though. Abuse was normal to me.

I've always believed deep down that love could not exist without pain—physical, emotional, psychological—but that's bullshit. I just didn't know any better because I've never seen anyone in a loving relationship that didn't have a daily dose of abuse—mainly verbal. I'm not only talking couples, I'm talking families, brother, sisters. All relationships.

I really like the book. I understand my family better and why I made the same mistakes without realizing it. I need to learn how to stop the vicious cycle of abuse. I want to teach my son that love doesn't have to hurt to be real. That disrespect shouldn't be expected from someone who loves you. I want to teach him to be a good man, but first I need to learn how to define what a good man is. I've always thought my father was a good man, but he is flawed and mistreats my mother regularly. I mean, they talk to each other fucked-up, but they will never leave each other. It's crazy because that's one of the reasons I thought he was good, because, despite all the fights, he never left, and most of my friends grew up without a dad.

I've been praying a lot more and reading the Bible. I'm striving for peace, and it's working. I'm taking care of a few plants, and I'm singing to them now. Don't laugh—I know it sounds silly, but it works. They are growing and green, so green they look fake. The light I carry inside me is feeding them, and it shows.

They also started an ESL class twice a week. I still tutor

187

some of the girls, and they are getting better at English every day. I'm also trying to start a GED class. I offered to teach the class; I'm just waiting to get approved by the educational director. I found a Colombian lady who is good at math, so we plan on teaming up to help the girls. I'm reading two books that will help me teach students who are not English speakers. Most of the girls who want help with the GED prep speak Spanish. Many came to America in their early teens and have problems mastering either language. Of course, many understand Spanish better than English, but not enough to take the GED in Spanish. It's a little frustrating because I wonder what they were doing in school all this time. Many got placed in bilingual classes, and many were passed for good behavior. These books are teaching me common problems to look out for. I can't wait to teach them how to write an essay. I love teaching the basic essay format. I like the way the writer lights up when they learn how to write an introduction and when they really get the meaning of a thesis statement. It's such a cool experience; it's like watching them communicate on paper with confidence. I'll let you know how and if they let me start the class.

Remember the pregnant girl? Well, she had the baby. She was able to spend two days with him. The poor girl had a C-section. When she came back, everyone tried to help out. I eventually got around to asking her about the experience, and she told me how nice the officers were to her, and how some of them even carried the baby. I asked her what was the first thing she said, and she shocked me with, *Is the baby light-skin?* And yes, she's a beautiful African American girl with caramel skin. I didn't question why she asked that question because I didn't want to irritate or offend her. I immediately thought about you, and I thought about my birthing experience. When I gave birth, my main concern was if the baby was okay; color wasn't an issue. I also used the journal you sent to write a response piece to your piece about almost shooting old boy. I will mail it next week. I will write again soon!

Lxxxx

CODA

On the 2 train and everybody plugged in. Eardrums occupied with sound, tuning out the world, if only for moment. The rails create a dawdling, meditative drone: entering and exiting stations, the streaming lights passing—first quickly, and then not at all. Train cars snaking along the third rail's curve and, for a split second, there is a glimpse of plugged-in people in the cars farther up. Saturday night, and I'm traveling from Harlem to the Metropolitan Detention Center in Brooklyn, which is a federal holding facility for people awaiting sentencing. At precisely 7:00 p.m. eastern standard time, I will stand on the corner of 23rd Street and 3rd Avenue in front of the twenty-four-hour video store and vigorously wave to Lxxxx, who will be staring down from the fourth-floor window at our predetermined time.

True, our lives intersected because of prison, but then, too, we've been baptized to these inglorious streets through trial and error, and we know that memory eats at the brain until there's nothing left but the act to dwell in. You and the act: memory and (re) memory. Our correspondence and conversations over the past year have been intellectual and stimulating—sometimes a little hood, sometimes a little confessional. In many ways, she is helping me deal and cope with the guilt, the never having forgiven myself for those memories I formed in the streets. I have never really taken the time to enjoy my achievements. Maybe it's because I always felt I should have been doing these things all my life. Lxxxx's predicament brought me back to Roxbury and trying to figure out the magical lexicon that would teach me to say I'm sorry. Our letters remind me of my time in Montgomery County Detention Center when I had to write down the things that had been the most painful in my life. She has made me take a deeper look at myself, and for that I am thankful. I can only hope that I have done the same for her.

In the winter, just before spring, I often reflect on my old college friend Jesse James Jackson. The repetitive winds of February and March recall his once-incessant laughter. His early death was inevitable insofar as one cannot escape the history one is destined to make. Jesse's murder presented life as tangible and tactile. I could touch it with my fingertips, and damned if it didn't touch me back.

My friend died alone in a bathtub, shot and then electrocuted.

So many times, I have placed myself in that bathtub, covered with water, bullet holes tunneled inside my head; and the moment the iron is thrown in, the body jolts alive one more time, and then, lights out. Items extracted from death: twenty thousand dollars, five kilograms of cocaine, and five pounds of marijuana. For Whip and Radar who pulled the trigger and threw the iron, a human being's life seemed a fair exchange.

Jesse was the first man I knew to die by the bullet. Drugs create an alternate reality, and in mine, he was one of many heroic figures. Maybe it's twisted, but what other memory I got? This is the only one I know. I can't reimagine images and events like they didn't occur. When you come out on the other side of the tunnel toward the light, are your friends still your friends? Am I still that same person called Hook? Do I get to claim the laughter of my youth? It almost doesn't seem fair. And if I am honest with myself, there were some nights I did wish to kiss this world goodbye. Many nights I did not want to breathe or go on, yet something willed me through the onyx of never-ending dead ends and false beginnings. The stop-and-start-all-over-again became routine. I was almost afraid of the steady and the sure, the slow money.

Most of the people I associate with today would not understand the sense of belonging a person incarcerated feels knowing someone made the trek from Manhattan to Brooklyn to stand on a corner and *wave like you just don't care.* However, it means the world to Lxxxx, and I know this. It perhaps means the world to all the ladies on Lxxxx's floor who are going through their own individual isolation and can witness her smile. *Life is made up of the small things.* I cannot help but think back to when I was in Baltimore County waiting to be shipped to Roxbury to begin my bid. From my cell window, I could see life pass me by, and no one knew I was watching. I didn't matter in the grand scheme of society. The local men from Baltimore would have friends and relatives come by and wave, and that made them feel connected, loved. Each night I went to sleep with an emptiness knowing there would be no one waving for me. And I wanted someone to, desperately.

Twenty-third Street could really be 9th Street in Northwest DC. Struggle is written all over the edifices of the storefronts; nothing here speaks of hope. This is where they put the prisons, so the landscape becomes one big blur of confinement, both monetary and physical. I know this place because they are all the same: buildings slightly run-down and full of people who aren't allowed to catch the spirit of Western civilization. These are the people I broke bread with; this is the place I came out of, alive. I know now I damaged myself, hopefully not beyond repair. And there is a fine mist of rain now, and perhaps I'm crying, too, but I can't tell. It's all coming together so fast—rapidly—the emotions, the memories. It's a slow walk, and I'm taking my sweet time, soaking up the bodega, the sound of kids riding mountain bikes down the side-street, the Chinese proprietor waiting for the next customer to walk through his door for a to-go order.

My phone vibrates, and it's a text from my boy Tyehimba Jess. After I wave to Lxxxx, I will meet Tye on 25th and 4th for a bite to eat. Eight years ago, I met Tye just after he'd won the National Poetry Series Book Award for his work on the blues musician Leadbelly. Later, at Chicago State, Tye would offer valuable feedback that would help shape my first book. Tye is a reminder of how everything around me is changing. I've tried to reimagine people, places, and my environment. Tye is a new kind of friend—the kind that inspires good instead of evil. I want to tell him that waving right now is more important than any book I have or will ever write, that there is someone in the world right now who needs to feel like she belongs.

It's 6:55 p.m., and I'm early. The detention center is next to the Bronx Queens Expressway, and I'm wondering what significance this might hold to the women who watch cars travel back and forth during any given day. I am sure they use the BQE as an escape mechanism, a way to imagine outside of themselves. I'm not sure where I should position myself or what angle would be best, so I move down by the video store and lean back on the old brick structure. Mist still coming down softly, and I have to wipe my eyes again. There is someone up there that needs to get out and cannot. The phone is ringing, and it's a blocked number, which means I know who the number belongs to. I answer the phone and press five, which you have to do if you want to accept a call from a federal inmate, and Lxxxx is like, *Oh my God, I can see you!* I'm smiling, and I wave and wave, and then wave again. We are laughing now, tripping on the phone like this is a regular prison visit. Lxxxx has to save minutes to talk with her son and other family members, so as much as I would like to stand in the droning mist and kick it, I know we have to say goodbye. But before we do, she's like, *Wait, let me get one more good look at you.* She hangs up and I stand where I am for another three minutes, leaning against the video store, thinking about my time in

Baltimore, and then I head down 3rd Avenue into an unknown future filled with new possibilities.

Eight million stories in New York City; this is mine.

ACKNOWLEDGEMENTS

This is a work of creative nonfiction. The events and experiences detailed are true and have been faithfully rendered as I remember them, to the best of my ability. Some names have been changed or altered to protect the privacy of certain individuals.

Special thanks to the following publications where portions or parts of this memoir were published: *Black Renaissance Noire*, Vol. 13 Issue: 2/3 (2013); *The Truth About the Fact: International Journal of Literary Nonfiction*, Vol. VII Issue: 1 (2012); *Pine Mountain Sand & Gravel: Contemporary Appalachian Literature*, Issue: 15 (2012); *Motif V2 Come What May: An Anthology of Writings About Chance*, Motes Books, (2010). The prison sections appear first in chapbook form as *Roxbury* from Kattywompus Press (2013).

I'd like to thank Becky Thompson, my sister from another mother, for her many reads and criticisms, how she fought hard for Lxxxx's voice to be heard. Thanks to Dwayne Betts, my brother from another mother, for the many reads and advice. Also, without Sammy Greenspan, I would have never been able to navigate the Roxbury sections. Other readers who I owe debt and gratitude to are DaMaris Hill, April Gibson (the world ain't ready, but you are!), Judith Katz, Monica Ong, James Cherry, Sally Ann Hard, Jeanie Thompson, Antoinette Brim, Adrienne Christian, Leola Dublin McMillan, and Lejohn Poole. Thank you.

Special thanks to Derrick Harriell, Patrick Rosal, Willie Perdomo, Frank X Walker, Roger Bonair Agard, Kim Coleman Foote, John Murillo, Hallie Hobson, Amanda Johnston, Linda Susan Jackson, Alexa Muñoz, Tressa Jones, and Patrick Oliver for inspiration, your ear, and friendship.

To Steak Daddy, Moon, Shell, G-Money, and Black—we been through the fire and back about five times. Maybe it's the memories that shape who we are to become. Without our collective memories, this book would have never been possible. Others that fall in this category: Jo-Jo, Debbie, Pepper, Deena, John Glenn, Joe, Lilton, Bibio, Andy, Steve, Rock, Bumshell, Lulu, Suga, Chocolate, Crip, Beanie, Carl Johnson, Doug Ellis, Lacy Robinson, Cat Daddy, Dale Harris, Dollar Bill, Tony

Jones, Mark Johnson, Dino Lyons, Whoopie, and Reginald Craig.

A big thank you to the staff at Augury Books for their belief in this project. Special thanks to my content editor, Kate Angus, who saw everything I could not see and made the difficult decisions when I could not. There are few editors/presses left in this current literary landscape that really invest in a writer's work, but Kate and Augury are that rare exception. Much gratitude.

I'm grateful to the National Endowment for the Arts, Birmingham Civil Rights Institute, University of New Haven, Alabama Writers' Forum, Cave Canem, Say it Loud! Readers and Writers, and the Gwendolyn Brooks Center for Black Literature and Creative Writing, for support, guidance, and encouragement.

Many thanks to Minerva Delancey of Hatchet Bay, Eleuthera for giving me the time and space to write by the sea every morning, to reimagine what I once saw. If your eyes could tell a story. Thank you Gina and Francis, proprietors of The Front Porch in Hatchet Bay, Eleuthera, a lovely restaurant nestled in a cove where I spent many evenings shaping the contents of this book. The best cracked conch diner in the Caribbean.

To those I carried the homeless stick with—I will never forget you. To those I hurt along the way—I will never be able to apologize enough. I know, some things I have to live with forever. Forgive me. I'm truly sorry.

Most importantly, I would like to thank Clarence and Eunice Horton for loving me when I could not love myself. Lesli Wallace, you are the best sister ever! Greg Leah and LaShondra Sutherlin, you guys are my rock, my balance. You make the world sane.

And lastly, *Hook* would not be possible if it were not for Linda Perez from Bronx, New York. Thank you for lending your words, your voice, your "gut" to help shape this project. I wish nothing but the best for you and your son. The door is open and you got next. Thank you, Linda.

Randall Horton
Harlem, New York, February 20, 2015

ABOUT THE AUTHOR

Randall Horton is the recipient of the Gwendolyn Brooks Poetry Award, the Bea González Poetry Award, and a National Endowment for the Arts Fellowship in Literature. His previous work includes the poetry collection *Pitch Dark Anarchy* (Triquarterly/Northwestern University Press, 2013). Horton serves on the board of directors for Pen America's Pen Prison Writing Program and teaches at the University of New Haven. He is a Cave Canem Fellow and a member of both the Affrilachian Poets and the experimental performance group Heroes are Gang Leaders. Horton is also a senior editor at Willow Brooks, an independent literary press he helped found in 2006. Originally from Birmingham, Alabama, he now resides in Harlem, New York.

Made in the USA
San Bernardino, CA
13 August 2018